DIAMOND

ALSO BY DAWN RAE DOWNTON

Seldom (2001)

DIAMOND

A MEMOIR OF 100 DAYS

DAWN RAE DOWNTON

M&S

National Library of Canada Cataloguing in Publication

. Downton, Dawn Rae, 1956–
Diamond: a memoir of 100 days / Dawn Rae Downton.

ISBN 0-7710-2829-6

I. Downton, Dawn Rae, 1956– – Friends and associates. 2. Diamond (N.S.)
– Biography. 3. Cancer – Patients – Nova Scotia – Biography. I. Title.

FC2349.D52Z49 2003   971.6'13   C2002-905635-7
FI039.5.D52D69 2003

We acknowledge the financial support of the Government of Canada through
the Book Publishing Industry Development Program and that of the
Government of Ontario through the Ontario Media Development Corporation's
Ontario Book Initiative. We further acknowledge the support of the Canada
Council for the Arts and the Ontario Arts Council for our publishing program.

Typeset in Sabon by M&S, Toronto
Printed and bound in Canada

McClelland & Stewart Ltd.
The Canadian Publishers
481 University Avenue
Toronto, Ontario
M5G 2E9
www.mcclelland.com

I 2 3 4 5   07 06 05 04 03

For Carol
vita brevis

I could give all to Time except – except
What I myself have held. But why declare
the things forbidden that while the Customs slept
I have crossed to Safety with? For I am There,
And what I would not part with I have kept.

– Robert Frost

Hope is the thing with feathers that perches in the soul.

– Emily Dickinson

[ONE]

Toto, We're Not in Kansas Any More

The farm lies along the Diamond Road, in the settlement of Diamond. That's what everyone says, at least, and one road sign points to it. But only one. If Diamond's here at all, you come upon it only from the east, driving up past the village to the turnoff from the 256. There's no sign in the opposite direction. Sign or no sign, we drive up and down the road to Diamond, and we never find it.

We hear the name bandied about by the locals. They're insiders who speak a code all their own, and while it shuts us out, it gives us hope that our home is there to be found. Someone at a neighbour's gathering calls it "the Diamond," as in, *You live in the Diamond? Floyd, these are the folks who just moved to the Diamond.*

With a little patience, the heart of Diamond can be found, a local historian has promised in a time-worn edition of the community newspaper. His little joke is to write and write in service to the solution of some mystery, and yet say almost nothing. He's like a deejay, sampling melodies that come up empty. *There is a small community tucked away among the great rolling hills of Pictou County,* he writes, theme and variation:

> *It carries a name, although not too unusual, that has caused a great deal of speculation as to its origin. The place is the pretty rural spot known as Diamond. It lies west of West Branch and east of Scotsburn, and it seems almost lost among the many picturesque, winding roads that criss-cross the section in every direction. Diamond lies in a fertile farming and lumbering district, but by no stretch of the imagination can it be suggested that there are diamonds there. The area does not lie in a diamond shape, formed by either the contours of the land or the small river that winds through the valley. There are no coal seams in the section that would suggest the name of black diamond, such as would be the case in many coal mining districts. While the pioneers to this section might have been "diamonds in the rough," that was not the reason.*

And so we never find it, except for an old burial site and a stream winding down B's topographical maps: *Diamond Cemetery, Diamond R.* Just short of the dilapidated wooden bridge over *Diamond R.*, there's a small wedge of cleared land where a schoolhouse once stood. It sported a diamond-shaped window in the peak of the roof, high over the front door: we know this from weathered old photographs. Mullioned to match the little diamond, several long, imposing sash windows underneath it, at ground level, march their way across the front and down the side of the school that faces the camera. A young marm in a broad-brimmed hat and a shirtwaist leans in the doorway, an inscrutable half-smile on her face. Her arms are crossed. She's the Diamond Mona Lisa, pensive or just plain bored as she considers her charges on the lawn in front of her. They're lined up for the camera according to height, six little girls in plaid seersucker dresses and ankle socks. They have bows in their hair; one has a sash at her waist. They're eager, shy.

Where are the boys? And where are all the older kids? Are they out of school already, working the fields? In the midst of such hard living nearly a century ago, the diamond-shaped window in the girls-only schoolhouse must have seemed an opulent, totemic thing. People say it gave the place a name. Everyone knows. No one knows for sure.

Otherwise, names are missing all around, or else they're piled on thick. The Diamond Road has two signs on it. There's → DIAMOND at the intersection; and then, once you make the turn, LOGANVILLE ROAD. His schoolbus turns around on the road at the Diamond, Daniel-from-next-door says casually. He's the neighbour's boy, eleven years old and sharp as a tack. He's only just moved here too. Listening to him toss off the local lore, I'm chagrined as any adult handed a solved Rubik's cube by a little kid.

Why can't we figure this out? Where does the Diamond Road end and the Loganville Road begin? Charlie is the kind of guy we ask things of, so we ask him. He's our age. He won't make us feel we should go out with the trash.

"Oh, roundabout the bridge."

"Why does it change there?"

"Well, because it does."

The farm itself, three miles down the Diamond Road, is manifest enough. You can't miss it, we tell everyone; and you can't. The long, lumbering farmhouse lies nestled in maples, elms, and ash at the end of a five-hundred-foot stretch of a treed gravel driveway. The house and its two barns are abutted on all sides by a large parcel of some of the best fields in the county, sutured together with a small brook. There's sixty acres of fields, level and fenced, easy of access and nearly two hundred years old, surrounded by another forty-seven acres of forest that's older still. This is Diamond Farm. But Diamond, the place, doesn't really exist. So says B after days of looking, as he noses the car down the driveway to the farm after another fruitless drive up and down the Diamond Road. The one sign points to it, the maps attest to it, at the bridge it ends, and Daniel-from-next-door marks it in his shining mind – but no one's ever seen it.

Maybe it's like Brigadoon. We'll just wait a hundred years, then the mists will clear and we'll see it, rising through a buttery haze on which crests a stirring chorus of Scots brogues. "How are things in Glocca Morra?"

✎

Not good, it turns out. The news from Carol is dreadful, in fact: cancer in her bowel. Then, two days later, an ultrasound shows it's travelled to her liver, and a CT says the liver is now more tumour than liver. That bad taste in her mouth she's been having all summer will grow; the bile will rise. She'll stop eating. When she dies, she'll have wasted away, literally starved to death.

We arrived home the week before, B and I, on the tail end of a tropical storm. In Nova Scotia, late-summer gales aren't so rare. They slam themselves into the south coast on the damp, stifling edge of the season, uprooting trees and dispatching roofs. In the midst of this one, I thought of Sylvia Plath surveying her grandmother's yard in the aftermath of a hurricane. "The devastation," she wrote, "was all one could have hoped."

Waiting out the storm delayed us, and it raged on anyway. It was well after dark when we drove up from the city to our new place, and then it wasn't just dark, it was pitch. One of the things I'd have to get used to was the utter darkness of the country at night. In Vancouver, there'd been no country, and so much city light and noise round the clock that there'd been no night to speak of either.

Rain sliced sideways past our windshield. Our lights picked out a highway sign: ROUGH SECTION NEXT   KM. Someone had forgotten to fill in a number, or had thought better of it. All I could think of was Carol.

I've been away two years, back home six days. She's my familiar, my closest friend. Has been for ten years. If I were writing it in a novel, the heroine's plane would be met by police. The heroine's darlings, the ones she hadn't seen for years, the ones doting on her every word in her letters or down a long-distance line, the ones racing down the highway to meet her, laden with gifts – they would have been wiped out in an accident on the way.

⌣

Diamond doesn't exist – it's easy for B to say. But I have to believe in it. It has to exist. I brought us here, after all, and since everything I'd counted on so far has fallen apart, some things had still better turn out right.

Meanwhile, we'll have to make do with our ordinary lives, our mortal romance, our daffy ducks, our well problems. Wait and hope long enough, though, and one day Lerner and Loewe will tuck themselves under the edges of our sleep, massed chorus and violins and all life's hope and glory building as we wake.

In *Brigadoon*, there's Tommy Albright, Jeff Douglas, Fiona Campbell: Gene Kelly, Van Johnson, Cyd Charisse. Van Johnson's the cynical one, but Gene Kelly as Tommy Albright – with a name like that, he's the one to fall in love and cause all the trouble.

Events at Brigadoon are set in motion when two Americans on a hunting trip in the Scottish highlands stumble on the tiny village – the one day in 36,524 it throws off its century of sleep. Fine dress, fine manners, *if you please, sirs* and *thank yous* – Tommy and Jeff seem to have stepped into the past.

And they have, literally. The village was enchanted centuries before. It's stopped in time, invisible – but for one special day every hundred years, when it appears to outsiders. They can even go in and visit. Mr. Lundie, Brigadoon's sage old schoolmaster, discloses the town's secret. Long before, the town minister had sacrificed himself so that Brigadoon would sleep a hundred years at a time, so that it would live on eternally, unaffected by the ills of the world.

But now here are two of them, fresh from New York.

Tommy falls in love with the bonny Brigadoonian Fiona. But when a local leaves, the entire town does too. If Fiona goes off with Tommy, she'll break Brigadoon's ancient enchantment and doom everyone in it. It will vanish forever.

Tommy thinks it over. Does he stay in Brigadoon with his love, and abandon his life in New York? He's left a fiancée behind there. He returns home out of duty but he's miserable, having compromised true love for hypocrisy. Breaking his engagement, he rushes back to the Scottish highlands, poking through the thistle and the heather, searching the mists for Brigadoon.

Magically, it reappears. How about that?

Wise old Mr. Lundie explains it all. "If you love someone, anything's possible – even miracles."

·~

Martha Stewart may say it soon enough, so let me say it first: Miracles are a good thing, so long as they get you what you want.

According to the Irish legend, if you go to Ireland and kiss an old stone in the wall of Blarney Castle, triangular, about twenty feet from the top of the wall and difficult of access, a gift of eloquence and persuasion dusts your tongue like confectioner's sugar, and gets you anything you want.

So far, our house is falling apart, the well water's foul, and my best friend's leaving against her will, never to return. There's another friend too, the one who brought us to this place, and though that friend's not dying the friendship is. On top of all this, we can't even find the place where we live. We're not doing so well, that's certain; every day brings a new body count. *With a little patience, the heart of Diamond can be found.* Really? When it comes to getting what we want, I wonder how much we're going to be handicapped here in Diamond, in Scottish country where the Scots made landfall on the good ship *Hector* and the Irish did not. What did the ancestral Scots do for miracles? Did they just realize God was agin' 'em from the start? Were they a talkative bunch, or did they go quietly about their landing and settling, an entire culture ground down at the heels from God's disfavour?

Did they ever sing anything remotely like "How are things in Glocca Morra?"

Me, I've piped down over the years, grown quiet. Back on the west coast, B once visited the Vancouver Aquarium with his kids.

"Are they boy fish or girl fish?" his son asked, in front of a tank of Japanese carp.

"Both," said B. He pointed. "But that one's a girl."

"How can you tell?"

"Its mouth is open."

B tells me his little joke hopefully, nearly plaintively. He repeats it now and then, to see if he can get a rise, even a smile. But the humour's left me and the blarney too. I wear more black and remark on things less. Talk seems to have less point than it did when I was twenty, thirty; or maybe I've just used up my allotment of observations and findings, as if, like the eggs in my ovaries, I've been born with a finite number and shouldn't have wasted them earlier in life. The strong, silent type, B himself says little at the best of times. He's chatty only on morphine or lack of sleep. *I feel the light around me*, he says then. *I feel the light. Do you feel it?* When I sit by him in Emergency while he passes his annual kidney stone, when I pick him up from red-eye flights home, then he's positively garrulous.

Is eloquence what's wanted here, for Carol? Who could I persuade? Of what? Charlie's come over with caulking and a ladder. "It's not good," I tell him, and then the details, and we stand together and stare out across the fields. He's just lost his father, who was old. Wind blows in our faces. It's a cold, cold day.

"There's nothing to say," he tells me finally. He's right. And he's wrong.

Perhaps the most talked-about death of all time, perhaps also the most miraculous but for Bobby Ewing's on *Dallas*, Christ's death on the cross seems the least detailed in the telling. The story is chaste in its essential elements, even spartan. Wouldn't it have been better for Matthew, Mark, Luke *et al.* to go all out, make a sales pitch? *Death on Cross Saves World*, read all about it! But there's no long, considered account, few details, no narrative of the whole, step-by-step, minute-by-minute, blow-by-blow. Perhaps, as Calvin put it, "these matters call for secret meditation, rather than for the ornament of words."

Stories happen only to people who can tell them, Thucydides is supposed to have said. Well, what of my brooding and hovering? What can I make of this? It's not like there can be a lot of suspense to terminal cancer; everyone sees at the outset just how it will end. What's to tell? What's the story, what's at stake? Why shuffle these proceedings like a deck of cards, forever palming the ace of spades? What kind of story is that, what sleight of hand?

My story is like the Ancient Mariner's, really the only story any of us ever tells: *I was not always as you see me now.* It's Carol's story too: she was not always as you see her here.

We were *best friends*. It's the great hope of childhood: that I might fit into you, and you into me, and the rest of these jokers can get lost. It's rare that it happens at all; rarer still that it lasts any time. But we did something even rarer, Carol and me. We didn't meet as children and become best friends. We were all grown up.

What drew us together was recognition. She recognized me; I recognized her. We unearthed each other.

I met her when she took up a new job. I had a similar one elsewhere in the place, and we were going to be colleagues. She was wearing a spanking navy suit over a pert white blouse with a lace collar. The skirt of the suit had knife-pleats. She was dark and it all looked good on her, smart rather than severe. That was the thing about Carol – she was like Nancy Drew's friend Bess Marvin, particular about her clothes. Bess always looked like she'd stepped out of a bandbox, whatever that was. Carol dressed immaculately,

looked smart. She *was* smart. She was more like Nancy Drew than
Bess in the end, she was that smart. Always the kick, never the sidekick. Immaculate, consummate. Perfect, or near enough. There
were people who didn't like her for it. I wasn't one of them.

> *Nancy lives with her dad in a big house in a rich neighbour-
> hood in the city of River Heights. She has a huge wardrobe,
> two good friends, a nice boyfriend, and her own car, a road-
> ster. She is capable in nearly every way, is good at sports, and
> belongs to the River Heights Country Club, where she plays
> golf and tennis. Nancy is titian-haired, sixteen, and travels a
> lot. She doesn't have to go to school. She is very independent,
> brave, and kind. Since the death of her mother, she helps the
> housekeeper, Mrs. Gruen, in running the house. Nancy is a
> brilliant amateur detective, forever finding mysteries to solve,
> together with her family, her boyfriend, and her friends.*

I took her hand the day I met her, pressed it. "Congratulations," I
said. "Or commiserations." These were rotten jobs we were in.

Her hand pressed back. Her dark eyes widened. She'd spotted
me. "Or both," she smiled. She already seemed to know it.

We weren't a predictable match, more like the strange attrac-
tors of chaos theory than soulmates in some destined collision. On
the job, she took things to heart, and while I was intense I was
seldom serious. We understood each other, but rarely got het up
over the same things. I'd been there longer than she had, and I
cared little about it any more. She was stung by the injustices she
ran into, the ones that by then I swept up each morning and threw
in my dust heap. At work, I became a kind of mentor.

She was pristine, black and white; I was fair, wore a lot of pink, and had bad habits and a mouth. The worse that job got, the more mouth I had. She liked a laugh but hated gallows humour. She worried that things might be in bad taste; I worried that they might not.

We came from different backgrounds. She had kids, a reliable husband who, like God, was an Englishman. *Ned Nickerson is Nancy's boyfriend. He plays three sports – football, basketball, and baseball. He adores Nancy.* She had a Good Housekeeping home with area rugs and dark wood and dinner parties. *Nancy has a very beautiful home – a large brick house away from the street with a nice garden surround.* I had no kids and, back then, an angry husband who drank too much. Because he was seldom there, I made a sanctuary of my home, admitting next to no one. Her upbringing was British and traditional, and while not exactly privileged it was not exactly poor. Mine was colonial, fractured, fatherless, bankrupt. The government considered me an orphan and sent my mother a Widow's and Orphan's Benefit. I was always scrambling for something.

Still, she'd fought enough battles in her life to recognize the style of the scrapper. She brought my method finesse and grace. She put manners on my occasional brat; she became a kind of mentor. She was like a heroine out of Forster, not old or whitened or doddery like Adela Quested's wise old travelling companion, Mrs. Moore, in *A Passage to India* – not doddery at all, in fact – but for all the world a kind of Mrs. Wilcox at Howards End. Mrs. Moore, Mrs. Wilcox: the good die old in Forster, or at least, like Carol, they make it to middle age. But the young make a hash of things forever. It's the young we could do without.

Carol was like the first Mrs. Wilcox, the doomed one who's too fine, who has to be written out of the story in order to let the crass red dust of newness settle over the Empire, in order to let someone else, someone lesser, marry the widowed Mr. Wilcox and take over gauchely, strewing the hallowed paths of Howards End with decay. Carol was a dying breed, I knew that – but I never thought she would die; not really. What was I thinking? That she'd be grand, that's what. In her dignity, she'd be everlasting. She'd be the first Mrs. Wilcox always, coming down from London forever to open the country house, throwing open the French doors to the hay-meadow in back, causing all the red dust types to sneeze with hayfever. *Trail, trail, went her long dress over the sopping grass, and she came back with her hands full of the hay that was cut yesterday. . . . she kept on smelling it.*

Mrs. Wilcox may not have lasted, but this was real life, and I thought Carol would. I thought she was invincible. I came to see her cool and polish as shatterproof. It was a mistake that I've paid for, and will pay for some more.

Perhaps part of my penance, like the Mariner's, is to have to go over it and over it again. "There's nothing to be said," Charlie says. He's right, and he's wrong. Just leave it to me. I can inject the whole sad affair with dye to see what stands out. I can never just leave it alone.

You're welcome to write about this, she'd say to me when she was angry – at doctors, at her cancer, at her husband, John. But that's not what I'm doing, exactly.

It was just that I loved talking to her.

Is this her way to talk back?

Recounting the story of a death is just a ruse, a management technique. You tell yourself *this is how it was*, you tell yourself you've licked it, you've prevailed; you've even, in your way, flung your lifesavers out into the chop and rescued everybody at the end.

She's here, isn't she? you tell yourself. *Spit and polished. In some ways, better than she was in life.* You don't shut up, you can't. You go on and on. These fragments have I shored against my ruins.

She gets sick. She is fifty-five; she has two children who will mourn her and never stop mourning. She will have grandchildren who will never know her. Ever after, when I see her, the unornamented words of Ecclesiastes come to me: *Rejoice, O young man, in thy youth.* I keep them to myself. For her memorial service she wants the staple instead, *To every thing there is a season* . . . Andrea Bocelli and Sarah Brightman have been on the radio a lot with "Time to Say Goodbye" – maybe we could play a tape of that? Sondra, who sings beautifully, will sing something. Margot, who went through Anglican seminary almost to the end and knows how things go in a service, will oversee. Maybe the kids will want to get up and read something, Carol doesn't know. She wants me to say something, since I'm her only erudite friend. She likes erudition, quotes lots, the lofty stuff, despite her outrage in these dark, dark days. Camus said this, she tells me, fixing me with her stare: *In the midst of winter, I finally learned that there was in me an invincible summer.*

I couldn't say that if I stayed up all night, working at it. "Does it have to be erudite, what I say?" I'm worried. Carol has a stare that you can't wriggle out from under at the best of times, and these days it's more fixed than ever.

But she's looking at her watch to see if it's time for her breakthrough Dilaudid. She didn't notice I'd made a joke.

•‿

The Blarney Stone's too high up in the wall of Blarney Castle for anybody to kiss. God knows how the ancients did it. Nowadays, things have been made easier for tourists. A substitute stone has been provided, and it is promised to be as effective as the original.

But if I just had to have the real thing?

I could say that to B, and he wouldn't blink an eye. He's known me well all these years, and he knows I always have to have the real thing.

Only the best for my D, he'd say, and he'd lift me up for my kiss.

◦⸾

I lost another friend years ago, to AIDS. His partner, Richard, wore suits to the ICU every day. None of us on the deathwatch with him was to make plans, Richard said. No funeral arrangements, no lawyering. The day before Richard arrived, I brought in a lawyer to Max's bedside, to certify a list of last wishes he'd written out earlier, when he still could, on an art card. The lawyer drew up forms: where she indicated, Max signed with an X. The lawyer brought in a legal assistant to help witness those Xs, so that I wouldn't have to.

That had all been done, at Max's request, and then Richard arrived. Then, we weren't to speak of death at all. He'd made a deal with God, and we'd better do our bit to keep up our end. The deal? If God would save Max, then Richard would be good ever after: he'd be positive, he'd dress nice.

This – the reason for the fancy dress and the gag order – I found out on an elevator between the third and second floors of the hospital. Richard punched the STOP button and launched into his explanation. It was a lecture, a homily, about not giving up hope. Surely God wouldn't kill a guy in a suit.

"It's not Max in the suit," I said. Shock and grief were confusing all of us. Hope was confusing us too. *A shred of hope can fairly incapacitate a man*, says the writer Josephine Humphreys.

The elevator didn't stop when Richard punched the button. Does that happen only in movies? The doors opened and closed on the third floor, then the second. Nurses, families, patients in hospital-issue striped cotton robes and johnny shirts, cleaners with trolleys, they all got on and off. Richard kept pushing the button. We were still going down.

·

In a glass jar was placed one handful of crushed mint leaves, and three pinches of salt.

The jar was then filled with sweet wine and mixed.

The jar was then covered and set in a dark closet for three days.

After this time the mint leaves were strained out and laid on blotter paper to dry, which took a full day.

She ground up the dry mint leaves and placed them in a small cloth pouch.

She took a necklace that she wore and dipped it into the jar, and soaked it. She removed the necklace and this she placed wet round her neck, and the potion ran down her breast.

She then wet both hands and both wrists with the remainder of the potion, and this she poured over a flat stone where she had written the name of Pollard in charcoal.

*She poured the jar, and she laid her hands on the stone and
said these words three times, which were the words "Unto me
what is mine."*

*And then she went to the tavern and she sprinkled some of
the crushed leaves on the saddle of his horse and entering she
approached Pollard himself. He did not know her as the sister
of the man he had robbed, so he paid her no mind. She circled
him three times, dropping mint leaves in her path and some
in his ale. And when she left the tavern she cast the rest to
the wind.*

In New Orleans, a black hen's egg brings madness to him whose
name is written on it backwards. Take a black cat with a single
white paw, rub the paw against a vial in which you've mixed a
potion of jimson weed, sulphur, and honey, sip the stuff – you've
got a cure-all.

Black hens, black cats, white paws. In Louisiana, curses and
cures alike come in black and white.

I put a curse on someone once. It was red, not black and white.
Who knows, maybe I'd have done better to stick to monochrome.
I used a square of crimson silk unearthed from a remnant table in
Eaton's fabric department, a few raccoon hairs pilfered from the
hem of my mother's winter coat, some red candle wax melted and
dripped on the fur. The wax was my own innovation – blood
sacrifice seemed a useful thing, but not if it was going to have to
be my blood. Candle wax looked the part, or close enough.

From the woods behind her farm, the farm down the road from
Diamond where she lives still, Zelda brought the pièces de résis-
tance: bleached fragments of animal bone, a tooth that didn't look

human, and a bullet we called silver but which was stained, tinny, and dented.

She laid down the animal tooth, folded her hands across her chest. We didn't have anything from our victim-to-be. "It's *his* tooth we need," she complained. "Fingernail cuttings, at least. Some bit of DNA or something."

"Parings. In English murder mysteries, they call them nail parings. Agatha Christie, for instance. It's the bitten nails on the schoolgirl's body, but, in the wastebasket in her room, nail parings from the cabaret dancer in *The Body in the Lib* –"

"Right." She was waiting, not patient.

"Okay. How're we going to get his DNA?" It wasn't like my victim and I were Othello and Desdemona, sharing a bunk.

She was no longer listening. She was intent on arranging the ruined old bullet in the fragments of fur from my mother's coat.

"Never mind about his DNA," I told her. "It's what we say that matters. We need to be careful. The form and the language of magic is all important. One wrong word and it backfires on us." I was taking semiotics in grad school. You could barely speak to me any more.

"Well, what do we say?"

I had no idea. We used my TM mantra, which I'd discarded by grad school anyway. Grad school seemed to demand more in mental and spiritual armaments than those proffered by the Maharishi.

"We'll say *shirring*. It's a mantra. It's universal."

"Shirring? Like sewing? Smocking?"

"ShirRING. ShiRRRRRING."

We dripped our little pile of hair, tooth, bone, and bullet with red candle wax, bundled it up in the silk, and set it between us on my kitchen table. I'd been making soup; the room reeked of onions. Dishes overflowed the sink. The fluorescent fixture sputtered overhead, disapproving. We turned it off. For a moment we were in velvety, oniony dark. Then, a cigarette lighter, a cigarette end glowing on my side of the table.

I relit the candles on either side of the silk bundle. We stared into them.

Shirrrrrrring . . . Shirrrrrrring . . . .

We stuck at our incantation for twenty minutes, stopping once so I could light a new cigarette. Cross-eyed, hyperventilating, we got in the car and drove to the crime scene. Half a block away, we cut the lights and the engine and rolled to a stop – this for show only, since our man lived near a busy intersection lit with car and street lights everywhere. We scrambled from the car and threw our amulet under his front step.

My victim looked pale and ill betimes thereafter, according to reports, and within the year married a pretty girl, much his junior, who left him two months later. I imagined him dragged through divorce court, losing everything. I imagined him wandering his empty, echoing flat, red-eyed, at four in the morning, bleak, despondent, peeling his own fingernails, paring them to shreds. It was the best I could do.

As for me, I had the worst year of my life.

I should've stuck to black and white.

·‿

I'm used to getting what I want. Because it's always a fight, I usually prevail. I put on whatever armour there is. I persevere. I last into the final round. I do not fall from the ring. I bounce against the ropes. In me there is no invincible summer, just the plodding months year-round. I believe in sacrifice, in miracles, whatever wins the day. I'm not proud, I'm not picky – I'll take whatever helps my cause. I fight the fight. If I don't win, I make do, and I tell myself that I did.

My mother brought me up this way, and it's her victory and her fault.

We lived alone in a small town, the three of us, after we left my father and his money. Once, we drove past a county fair on our way home from doctors' appointments in the city, and my mother slowed down the old Vauxhall and turned into the parking lot. It was something she seldom did; alone with two small kids and no money, there was too much *looking after* and *fixing* and *dealing with* and *compensating for* choking her life to kick back and relax. We never even stopped at restaurants along the half-day drive; who could afford that? Instead, my mother brought a deepfryer full of crispy, browned chicken, which would sit at my feet on the floor, jammed against the front seat. She packed a plastic bag full of split rolls, already buttered, another bag of celery and carrot sticks, a Tupperware container of tomato wedges, a roll of paper towels, and a bag of wet washcloths for clean-up. We'd stop at a roadside field somewhere and eat, run off our steam a bit, pee behind the trees. My sister was a bit older, a bit faster. We'd streak around the fields, shrieking and laughing; she'd grab my ankles and fall on me, bringing me down. Our mother would smile and look off into the middle distance, thinking about schedules and bills. We travelled the way the poor travelled, third-class, but we were aired out and clean.

There we were, that day, at the fair. My sister and I stumbled around the grounds like aliens newly arrived on the planet. Everything was rich and wondrous, abundant. There were throngs of people, stands, games, food. Even the candy wrappers and the refuse on the ground had a kind of bounty to it. *All that stuff.* It was something we didn't see every day.

My sister threw a ball and won a stuffed monkey with a plastic face. She stared at it, at the unexpected turn in her fortunes. *I never win anything*, she said. We were only seven and eight, but we had no bounty in our lives and already we'd learned to say things like that.

The monkey paled even before we got all the way home. Its plastic face was thin and brittle, and she accidentally punched a fingernail right through its cheek. *It's cheap*, she said miserably, and threw it down on the back seat between us.

I picked it up, stroked the cheek, set it back on her lap. *It's beautiful*, I said. *You won it. It's a miracle.* I pretty well believed it.

I make do.

·~

In Brigadoon, there's a love story, a miracle, and a sacrifice. At one time, there were also witches. Lerner and Loewe's *Brigadoon* was probably based on the real Bridge o' Doon, an ancient thirteenth-century stone span in Alloway, Scotland. Alloway's the heart of Robbie Burns country, and Robbie Burns wrote about it. Tam o' Shanter fled over the Brig o' Doon on his horse, Meg, to escape the three witches pursuing him.

So this is where my mind goes, at Carol's news. To fighting the fight. To potions, to charms and double trouble, to eye of newt. Running from witches, running to them. Like Max's Richard in his suit, I'm punching buttons in the hospital elevator; I'm looking for the heart of Diamond. *Help, help. Can anyone hear?* I'm thinking prayers, negotiations with a God who likes to deal himself out of the hand. Anything to lift the sentence, unseal the doom, make it like it was before. Is this why people say over and over they wish there was something they could do – because they can't? Fate is just that indelible. *It is written.* The book snaps shut.

Not a spell, then. Not a curse, either – it's much graver to curse than to bless. But what's to bless here? No, I want something simple. I want her not to die. I'm sticking to black and white. I want things put back the way they were. I'm having trouble making do.

If you love somebody, anything's possible – even miracles. I want Mr. Lundie.

At Carol's dreadful news, my mind runs these laps. It doesn't always seem to come back.

The days are long. At night, wind shrieks round Diamond Farm. Somewhere in the New Testament, Jesus reminds the old sinner Nicodemus that *the wind bloweth where it listeth, and thou hearest the sound thereof, but canst not tell whence it cometh, and whither it goeth.* Not so on the Diamond Road. The wind races into northern Nova Scotia from the west and hurls itself round our place, half renovated and shivering to its bones. On it goes, then, down to the houses at Loganville. My friend Zelda used to call me during the winds. *Dawnio, I'm afraid the trees are going to fall right into my house.*

On the Prairies, people have to replace their roofs every five years because the nails rattle in their holes, widening them so that the shingles lift, slip their moorings, and fly away. There are Prairie towns that blame their high divorce rates on the wind. On the Diamond Road, at Loganville, people stay together, but it's said they've gone mad in the gales. We get heavy, heavy garbage cans. Once the bears come, driven from the woods by a summer

of feverish logging, we get heavier ones. When I put out the blue
bags at the end of the driveway, I tie them to the alders by the
mailbox so they won't blow away. Recyclable or not, it's as if I'm
losing so much that I still can't give anything up.

B likes the wind. He thinks it's cozy. "Just so long as we don't
wake up in the morning," he says, "and find the Wicked Witch of
the West sticking out from under the deck, feet first." He sees my
face. "Well, it could always bring us Mary Poppins."

He likes rain too, thinks snow flying horizontally past the
windows is romantic. Growing up in Norway, he never saw enough
sun to miss it. No doubt he's of Viking blood, genetically pro-
grammed for plunder in any weather.

Me, I don't think the wind is going to bring us Mary Poppins.
I'm worried we might not wake up at all. At night I have Cassandra
Dreams of impending doom. I fight the fight. I scream, I howl; my
voice is whipped away by wind, and no one can hear my warning.
Dream apartment buildings collapse around me, taller and bigger
each night. High-rises, tenements, skyscrapers, washing lines hanging from skyscraper windows. Skyscrapers don't have windows that
open, of course, but these are dream demolitions. My dream buildings don't just go down, they buckle under. A controlled collapse by
a demolition team is called shooting a building, as in *we're shooting
the Sears Tower tonight, in her dreams*. I hear the roar, see the dust
rolling out. Clouds of dust obliterate the washing lines. I see a tree
or two of Zelda's fly by, snapped like toothpicks from their roots.

I awake from a windy night a different person. I'm maddened;
I've had a sudden change of personality, like Phineas Gage with a
railroad spike in his head. Some days, I fall apart. I'm on the sofa
with the newspaper. Out of the corner of my eye I see the china

cabinet go down, then the hutch holding the Rosenthal plates and the antique eggcups. The kitchen cupboards yawn from the wall and drop, spitting out Mason jars, coffee mugs, yellow split peas, and canned tomatoes. There's a distant roar, a rain of pasta, a haze of pasta dust. Porcelain fragments saunter slo-mo through the air. My Old Country Roses teapot from Royal Albert, the one my mother gave me with eight cups and saucers and a matching tiered plate for petit fours, bounces twice before it shatters.

I won't be surprised if the Hindenburg crashes and burns on our front lawn.

I say nothing to anyone. Years ago, under prolonged stress, I sat down beside a woman in a white angora sweater. She placed her arm on the table between us, and the Royale toilet tissue kittens rolled down her sleeve. I mentioned it to my doctor. Perhaps I imagined she'd say I was working too hard, I should slow down. Perhaps I thought we'd share a laugh. No such luck. She talked antidepressants, anxiolytics.

Perhaps now she'd just think I mean that the house is falling down around me, that it needs work. Perhaps she'd just say *you're a little down, a little stressed. Your best friend's dying, another one's dumped you.*

One day, I hear the roar, look up from my book, turn my head: the cupboards let go and a can comes straight for me. Once it hits me it'll be dented on one end, bulged on the other. It'll have to be thrown out. Things my mother taught me, and I remember them all at times like this. I'll be fabulous at surviving food poisoning, less so the loss of a friendship and another friend's death.

⁔

Diamonds. The Koh-i-noor. The Hope. The mythical Braganza. The Regent, the jewel in Louis Quinze's crown and later the stone in Bonaparte's sword. The Star of Africa, the world's largest cut diamond, hived off the one-and-a-half-pounder Cullinan along with eight other large stones and ninety-six small ones. The Florentine, the Sancy, the Excelsior, the Orloff in Moscow's Diamond Treasury. The Idol's Eye, the Cartier or Taylor-Burton, the Hortensia, all the famous stones. More often than not they're said to rain misfortune down on their owners. Look at Liz and Dick, after all.

It's what I'm feeling about our own little gem here, Diamond Farm.

But malign diamonds can be rehabilitated. The exotic Koh-i-noor, for instance, the diamond with the longest history. Its name means Mountain of Light, but it began life fireless, flat, a lumpy Mughal-cut stone. Only the Mountain's weight was impressive: 191 carats. With the annexing of the Punjab in the middle of the 1800s, the stone came to the British crown. Garrards of London recut it for Queen Victoria, to 109 carats of fire and brilliance.

So it lost a little weight, a few lumps. It also lost its hold on famine, misery, insanity, indigence, violent death: all these things it's said to have brought to the sultans, the rajahs and shahs who begged, borrowed, and ransacked for it. The Koh-i-noor languishes today as the centrepiece in the Queen Mum's 1937 coronation crown, mouldering under glass at the Tower of London while tourists queue around it.

Which one's the Hope Diamond? That's what they want to know.

It's the most notorious stone of them all, Louis Quatorze's vain Hope, colour of sapphires and the largest blue diamond known, even after it's cut and cut again, ending up a heart. Stolen during the French Revolution along with the Sancy, it resurfaced in 1830 in England, bought by the London banker Thomas Hope. Were he at it today, would Mr. Hope be buying Canary Wharf instead of gems, and doing just as badly? *A shred of hope can fairly incapacitate a man.* Maybe he should've stuck to black and white. All his family died in poverty, as did at least one subsequent owner. The Hope, the little blue broken heart, now lives in the Smithsonian – where, presumably, it conspires against no one.

Not all diamonds are good diamonds. Not all diamonds are a girl's best friend. Coal is called the black diamond, because both coal and diamonds are forms of carbon. An industrial diamond is a stone so flawed, impure, irregularly shaped, poorly coloured, or small as to have no value as a gem. The names of the three industrial grades are as blah as the stones themselves: *ballas*, *bort*, or just plain *carbonado*. Drilling bort is clumps of small round stones weighing on average .05 carats. Crushing bort, worse yet, is the lowest grade of diamond. It's ground down to grit, little better than bathroom Ajax, and used as an industrial polish.

Nature produces diamonds in many colours. Industrial grades run grey to black. Most of the stones that get used as gems are transparent and colourless, or nearly colourless. Colourless or pale-blue stones are most valued, and therefore most rare. Most gem diamonds are yellow-tinged. A "fancy" diamond radiates some colour. Red, blue, and green are rarest. Orange, violet, yellow, and yellow-green are commoner. A diamond isn't forever: hurl a bunch of atomic particles at yours, and you can recolour it.

Diamonds are weighed in carats (one carat weighs 200 milligrams) and points (a hundredth of a carat). A carat also isn't forever. Because its value has changed over time, there's confusion about the recorded weights of the famous stones. Most engagement rings are a carat or less – much less. Liz's rock was nearly seventy carats by modern measure, and as a fancy cut pear-shaped pendant it made a nice weight around her neck till she sold it to finance the construction of a hospital in Botswana. Prospective buyers had to pay a U.S.$2,500 non-refundable viewing fee. It went finally for nearly $3 million, reportedly to Saudi Arabia.

The diamond represents steadfast love, always has. But diamonds, it turns out, are not forever so much as they're forever changing. They get cut, they get stolen, they get found, sold, renamed; they get recoloured and revalued, they get turned into hospitals, their reputations get rehabilitated. How to change our diamond, the farm, the weight it makes around my neck? I haven't got the time for psychotherapy on this one, or the patience. Besides, there's not a psychiatrist to be seen for at least a hundred miles in any direction. We're in the boonies, and there aren't even any signs.

B thinks I'm asking what we'll renovate next. Gingerly, I mention my night terrors, my waking dreams.

Really? The house is falling down around us? I've hardly noticed. Thanks for pointing it out. He's more literal than usual; I'm more alone. He's preoccupied, tearing his hair out over the work to date, off in his own fog about what's still to be done. He knows Carol enough to know he likes her a lot. He knows nothing about Forster, Howards End, Mrs. Wilcox; he knows nothing even about Nancy Drew and Bess Marvin. He only sees someone who stands out.

And has now fallen down. He knows she's dying. He knows I'm afflicted.

"Do you remember the fly-swarming scene in *The Amityville Horror*?" I screw my fists into my eyes to hold in the tears.

"Upstairs, in the stuffy old back bedroom, how the houseflies kill the old priest who comes to bless the house?"

"They didn't kill him." B looks up from his stack of invoices from Home Hardware. He's got a glass of Scotch condensing on another stack, from Hector Building Supplies. "They didn't kill him; they only drove him out." B is an engineer; he's nothing if not precise. Now, he pulls at the glass, considers something more. "Better for Paddy they *should* have killed him."

"This isn't *The Amityville Horror*." It's become my role to defend the house.

"No. *That* house was nice." Our visit to Hector today has been the usual: crazy-making and at the same time memorable, as if we've been the only mortals ever to visit Venus but got stuck in the door of our landing craft. Today, B held up a cardboard box in one of the hardware aisles only to have the bottom fall out, dropping twenty-five pounds of nails on his foot. "I'll get 'em," Bunny whooped, running from the cash, and together we picked them up. Breathlessly, bending and scooping, Bunny told us about the bad day she was having anyway, involving her car and a cop. In Pictou, at Hector, there's always a story about a car and a cop.

Hector's a strange place. The first time we went, to get soffit, the manager looked at B suspiciously, then even more suspiciously at me. "You from town?" he asked, as if it were a distant galaxy. "You been watching them home improvement shows?" I've gone back with B repeatedly, to look for fasteners and caulking and drill bits and two-by-fours, and still I'm not done in by the place. Still, somehow, I hope to see him – the real Hector, Priam's eldest, the noble, most generous of all the Trojan chieftains, holding out against the rat Achilles among the toilet seats and the storm doors. But it's a building supplies store, after all, and B expects different things: that the guys in the warehouse out back will halve his eight-foot lengths with an electric saw, for instance, not a handsaw. They may have all the time in the world, but he doesn't, and he can't get over it. I don't go back with B to the warehouse much. The only thing there is boards, and guys standing around watching other guys cut them bit by bit with handsaws, and B watching all of them and fuming. But in the store – *now that you are gone, o Hector* – in the store, he should be swaggering in the paint aisle in his bronze helmet and breastplate, a life-sized cardboard cut-out, at least, plugging this week's markdown on exterior latex. Back in Troy, Hector was famous, he was really something, and when his ten holdout years were up and Achilles finally slew him, victor lashed what was left of victim to a chariot and dragged the body, gloating, three times around the walls of Troy. Here, while Pictou trades on his name, they've just forgotten him – Hector the valiant, the magnanimous, three times lucky except in death. It doesn't seem right. *Weave a circle round him thrice*, Bunny said to us today over the nails, or something like that: *I had to call him three times!* I shook my head; she was still mired in the story of the car and the cop. A Pictou County Mountie, off-duty, took a wrong turn in the liquor store parking lot and backed his Cavalier into Bunny's blue Sunfire, her pride and joy. The Mountie begged Bunny not to put the claim through her insurance – he'd be in trouble. Though she's not sure why except that he's a cop, Bunny agreed, only to find from the body shop that the job will cost $1,300. Not only will the Mountie not pay now, he won't even return her calls. *Three times I called him, Jeez.* Bunny is bereft about the nails, about those who Serve and Protect, who *maintien le droit*. Only today had she called the cops – *yeah, the Mounties*, she said, taking a breath, her eyes welling up as she looked at B, he has that kind of face – and now the cops were talking about it all as if she'd done something criminal, leaving the scene of an accident.

In the country, it's always like this, never like Troy. B lived in the country for a time some years ago, and he's been trying to get back ever since. He loves the country, hates city life. It's lucky for me he does, since I'm the one who dragged us here. I'm just evening the odds – that's what I say when he gets crusty after the latest well test comes back, still bad. I've brought us to a place where the mortgage payment is less than our monthly parking tab out west.

It's safe to throw our current misfortunes in his face, since he was the author of the earlier ones. The last dragging that was done, after all, was done by him. He dragged us to Vancouver for two years, where he had a job – and where I had to scramble for one too, to keep us afloat. My first year there felt like I'd landed on the moon, at a *Stargate* trader's stop of perpetual dark, heavy traffic and import prices. I'd wake up nights, sit up in bed and cry. The second year was the same as the first, like the verses in "Henery the Eighth I Am," just a little bit longer and a little bit worse.

Then Zelda called, breathlessly. Back home, just down the road from her, a farm was up for sale.

A farm. We didn't want to farm, but still we came, so that I could be near her. *Ballas, bort, carbonado.* The wind's shrieking in, the burdocks around the house reach up to our waists like a thicket in the Enchanted Forest, there's still no drinking water, and all my friends have gone away. *With a little patience, the heart of Diamond can be found.*

Hard to get B's attention, in the midst of all this, with my metaphysical problems. I'm on my own.

Diamond. The word's a variation of adamant, from the Greek *adamas*, invincible. Only a diamond cuts another diamond.

Adamant, formidable, invincible: I'll just get through the days till
the darkness goes. I'll have to be. Nothing else will cut it.

·⁓

The Tune stone dates from the fifth century AD and is the most
important of Norway's ancient inscribed rune monuments. Discovered in 1627 in the southeast part of the country, it's lately been
moved to Oslo nearby. It's a stone a few feet high that would reach
about up to my heart, and it's chiselled with runes vertically, on
both sides. It bears a message that scholars and translators can't
agree on, but it's clear that WiwaR carved the runes in memory of
WoduridaR. Whatever it means to say at the beginning, it ends by
describing how WoduridaR was celebrated after his death, though
he left no sons or male relatives, only three daughters.

Who was WoduridaR? Who was WiwaR? Were they partners,
the Rs, parents of the three daughter Rs? Were they friends? Why
is the beginning of the story muddy, ambiguous, but the ending
clear? Why does one bond endure, another break? What does it
demand, and what happens when it's lost? When do you build a
monument, and what should it say when you do?

We expect romances to fail. But not friendships. I didn't know
Zelda's and mine had failed until we were back. Before that there'd
been a letter from her, designed to hurt in every way, and just
because it was that kind of letter I thought little of it. *I hate you, I
hate you!* I scream in frustration – hardly ever, but I do. And I
pound B in the chest, and he catches my fists, wraps his own around
them, draws me in for a hug. *I love you too*, he says, and then there's
a pause, some coughing and sniffling, the beginning of a laugh.

She'd wanted us to buy Diamond jointly with Bill and Jim,

local farmers who were her friends. They'd get the land and the barns, we'd get the house. They could use the extra pasture, having taken on another forty head of cattle with nowhere to put them. Our lawyer hated the plan, so we gave Bill and Jim dibs on the whole thing and stood aside. They declined, told us to go ahead, and we did.

That's Bill and Jim's baler outside the window now. That's their hay in our barns. They get to cut the fields and use the barns, and we get the property kept up.

Ballas, bort, carbonado, Zelda said. We'd taken advantage of her friends.

We had? And wait a minute – wasn't I her friend?

Even if I could understand it, it wouldn't really matter now, and it wouldn't have mattered then. It wouldn't be what happened, really, a simple property dispute or a naive little plan gone off the rails. It wasn't the story of what happened between us. That story, the real story, happened earlier; I just didn't know it then. I still don't know it now. Translators and scholars will disagree on the beginning of the end, just where it flagged, just what was meant when I said *how are you?* and Zelda lied and said *fine*. When I said *how are we?* and she said *fine*.

Gradually, over the years, she'd become distant. Because she ran a farm herself I saw her more in winter than in summer, when she had more time, and I put the greyness about her down to the weather, the incessant snowfalls, the way she sometimes had to slide from the house to the barn across the snow, then climb down into the barn from the top of the latest drift that had snowed it in. Her farm shared winds with Diamond a mile or two to the west, cruel winds that would frost the surface of the drifts to an icy shine while she waited for the plough. She lived at the end of a small, forgotten side road, and after a storm the plough would be at least two days coming. People were always letting her down, that's how she felt, right down to the plough driver. But she didn't want help. She'd grown to scorn it. Once I took a shovel from her hand to help, and she took it back and turned away.

In twenty-five years we'd never had such a moment; now we were having them more and more.

How are you, Zelda? How are you really? I said that time. Her melancholy worried me.

I'm fine, she said.

She disliked most people, and they never knew. They saw the bright smile, the eager hello, and they never knew. She tolerated the Sunday drivers, the tire kickers, the ones who dropped by for tea at any hour because it was convenient for them and what in the world else would she be doing anyway, a single woman like that, alone?

I saw the growing grey. I felt the storm creeping between us. How would I know, I asked her eventually, if you were only tolerating me too?

Oh Dawnio, she said. *Oh Dawnio. Don't be silly.* The bright smile.

How are we really? I pressed her. *How are we really?*

We're fine, she said.

Diamonds didn't used to be cut at all. While today the world's big diamond producers are Botswana, South Africa, India, Brazil, Russia, Australia – and Arkansas, of all places – most of the really old stones came from India, where only God had the right to open one. Uncut, diamonds protected the kings who wore them. Cut them, and now you've done it, you've let in bad luck.

And so there's a sutra, something like a prayer, just for diamond cutters. A Q&A between the Buddha and a disciple, this "Perfection of Wisdom" sutra is a brief Mahayana Buddhist text first translated in China around AD 400 that remains hugely popular today. Clearly, folks like me have needed advice on the hard stuff for a very long time.

The Diamond Cutter sutra says that *things* and the separation between them are an illusion: *just as, in the vast ethereal sphere, stars and darkness, light and mirage, dew, foam, lightning and clouds emerge, become visible, and vanish again, like the features of a dream – so everything endowed with an individual shape is to be regarded.*

The Diamond Cutter sutra speaks in striking paradoxes, pairing things with their opposites. In other words, it sticks to black and white. The very way it's constructed, as a running list of blacks and their whites, shows that spiritual realization – escaping the illusion of *things* – depends on transcending the running pairs, the categories. For this reason, though it comes from a different Buddhist school, the Diamond Cutter sutra is considered very Zen.

What it has to do with diamond cutting I don't know. Perhaps the Buddha would explain it by resorting to a koan.

What is the sound of one diamond cleaving?
What is the sound of two friends leaving?

•⤳

When we came back from our two years out west, that was when I knew. I set aside unpacking for a day and drove up that small, forgotten side road. She was sitting in her front yard. I got out of the car, walked toward her. "Hey," I called.

She didn't even look in my direction.

⁕

My mother keeps a cookie tin on top of the silver chest in her dining room. It's an old one, square and worn at the corners. It's painted with wildflowers and one of those scripted verses you'd expect to find stitched into a sampler on the wall of your grandma's parlour:

> *Be to her virtues very kind*
> *But to her faults a little blind*

In the tin my mother keeps the accoutrements of aging: a blood-pressure cuff, white adhesive tape and surgical scissors, cotton balls, syringes for the B12 shots she gives herself monthly. It seems an odd, overly modern assortment for such an old tin. The message on the tin is odd too, quaint and fanciful in the age of loudmouths, squealers, and finger-pointers, of Ricki Lake and Geraldo.

Her virtues and her faults, it's how you'll have to think of Zelda now, if you can, my mother says.

I feel Bambi's rabbit Thumper pulling at my hem: *If you can't say anything nice, don't say anything at all.*

But there are plenty of good things to say about her. When you needed help, she was tireless; when you needed bolstering, she was effusive. She was funny and melancholy in mostly the right mix. Only in the grey days of February was she off, like the rest of us.

She was not a little whimsical. She put curses on my enemies with me. She wrapped up that ruined old rabbit bullet in the hem of my mother's fur coat. She made a private wishing spot for the two of us, on the lip of a brook that ran through the woods behind her farm. If I die an early death, scatter my ashes here, I implored her once.

Where can I be scattered now?

Don't worry, says B. Diamond will bury us both.

From Zelda's wishing spot, when she and I were younger, many a man was conjured. When we got older, many a man was sent away. She was always functionally single, unhappy in love. We did better together when I was too.

She had phobias that endeared her to me, the arachnophobe. She had phobias that I'd never heard of in anyone else – a dread of vomiting, for instance. It was a mystery to me how she'd brought up four kids; even when they were toddlers she'd run away if they called to her in the night with a stomach ache. If it was she who was sick she'd run outside and throw herself on the ground, in any weather, until her nausea passed – the grass in summer, the snow in winter. A holiday we'd planned was spoiled when rain set in the day we were to leave and she decided she couldn't face a ferry ride in high winds; someone might get seasick and throw up on her.

"We could sit far away from everyone," I coaxed.

"They might throw up in the room we're in."

"We could stay out on the deck the whole time."

"Dawnio. We'd be on the same *boat*."

I understood. It was how I felt about spiders. But she had fears that were tiresome too, even dangerous. Because she'd seen a high-speed accident as a child, she was the worst driver in the world, going half the speed limit on the highway. In the city she stopped dead at every intersection whether it had a stop sign or not. It was a wonder she didn't cause collisions.

I'd taught her to drive, or tried to, and it came back to haunt me. *Dawnio taught me*, she'd say to anyone complaining they'd be killed riding with her.

I told her she was a bad driver. Things had deteriorated from the days of her burgundy Austin Mini, the car she learned on and the one I drove, stuffed to the gills, to her Pictou farm when she moved there from Halifax. She followed in a truck with the bulk of her household effects. On moving day, her little daughter had come home early from school with a magic wand she'd made in art class from tinfoil, coloured paper, and streamers. We tied it to the radio antenna of the Mini. On the highway, it buckled in the wind, but the little car with the tinfoil sceptre became a vanguard to ride in on. It escorted the moving truck into Zelda's new life.

Moving day had been an auspicious day. Things had gone badly for her since. Another fresh start staled, another change of plans, more disappointment, more Legal Aid, more squabbles with a new husband who left and a family who didn't. And then I went and did it: on the highway one day when she stopped dead on an interchange and almost got us killed, I told her she was a bad driver. It was probably the beginning of my end. It was us against the world, that's how she saw it, and when her friends disagreed with her, when they smudged the image she held of herself, they were cast from the fold. She lacked the confidence to entertain questions.

The trust has broken down between us, she wrote at the end, after Bill and Jim and their forty new Holsteins, after the purchase of Diamond. But is it really like-mindedness friends need? The trust between them comes from brooking difference, from finding the nerve to disagree, finding the nerve not to walk away when it's you who's been disagreed with. I hadn't had that nerve myself, all those years, till now. This was the first time I'd openly disagreed with her. So many times I'd wanted to. All I wanted to say was, *Sweetie, that doesn't work for me.* But something had warned me off.

She could be peculiar, fey. She didn't believe in modern life, not in medicine, Touch-Tone telephones, microwaves, creature comforts. Lying on your ear was the way to treat earache. If the kid didn't finish all his antibiotic mixture – *really, why put all that stuff in your body if you don't have to* – you could add it to that bottle in the back of the fridge for next time. The sun was good for your skin; age, not sun, was responsible for crow's feet.

What *was* age, then? I'd ask. What caused it?

Age was just age, she said. She was out haying for weeks at the height of every summer and wouldn't wear sunglasses or sunscreen; she didn't believe in them either. But she dreaded looking old, and had more lotions and pricey creams than the beauty counters of Saks. It was odd to see them in her rickety house, where everything else spoke of scraping by. One of my last gifts to her was $80 worth of Ceramides capsules from Elizabeth Arden.

In ten or twenty years the locals will call her eccentric, dotty, just plain weird, *that crackpot old lady up on the hill.* She wouldn't have a phone jack in her house, nothing but a wired-in black dial phone on the wall, nothing but a wringer washer. The last time she'd been happy was as a small child in England, alone with her mother and her little brothers on a twelfth-century farm estate in the Midlands while her father worked at the University of Nottingham and stayed in town, bicycling back and forth on weekends. It was some pretty dream of an ascetic and stony past, and it's clamped on to her ever since.

Her hope was to live simply again, by which she meant stripping the plumbing and the wiring out of her house as soon as the last child was out on his own, pitching out the dial phone, dispatching even the chipped enamel wringer washer in favour of a washboard and a tub. A few years ago, when he exploded into the news, she felt an affinity for Ted Kaczynski, the Unabomber with the hate-on for technology. *Poor, poor thing*, she said. She always loved a man with a beard, a man who could chop wood and mend fences and handle a chainsaw. The Unabomber would detest phone jacks as much as she did.

For fifty years a hermit has lived without power or plumbing deep in the woods beyond Diamond, beyond Zelda's place, beyond Charlie's place. No one sees him much, except now and then when he lumbers down the road on his old bike. Other than that, people bring him things, food.

"What people?"

"I don't know," says Charlie. He turns the tea in his cup. "Albert's not exactly pleasant. You wouldn't want to spend time with him."

If I am pressed to say why I loved him, said Montaigne of his friend Etienne de la Boètie, *I feel it can only be explained by replying: "Because it was he; because it was me."*

So it isn't either of us any more, and I don't know what more can explain why we're no longer friends.

On one of the last visits I made to her, I discovered she'd taken pictures of the two of us out of their frames and crammed them into an old shoebox, stuffing them in among weathered family photos of great-great-grandparents, great-aunts in hats, young girls on old bikes, small boys in shorts standing beside iron gates – all people she didn't know but might one day remember, if she studied them hard enough.

Friendships wear out, that's all. The window's closed now, but I still stare out of it a lot, thinking of her. I wonder if she thinks of me.

⁓

At Diamond Farm, the wind continues to blow. B thinks we might get a wind report as part of a local weather forecast, so we look for a radio station in the white pages. They're easy to find, because all Canadian radio station call signs start with C, except in Newfoundland. In Newfoundland, they start with V.

"V?"

"A carryover from their colony days," B explains.

"A Viking colony? V for Viking?"

"Nah. V for Vanquish. The Vikings didn't do colonies. They weren't really into the colonial experience; they liked to get right in and right back out, all in a day's work. Those Swedes, now, *they'd* have had colonies. If they could've rowed, that is."

B has a Norwegian Viking somewhere back there, raiding and pillaging, on his family tree. He's sure of it. He loves to tell people about the vast billboard that towers over passengers coming through Heathrow: STATE BANK OF NORWAY – DOING BUSINESS IN THE U.K. SINCE 946 AD. As recently as his grandfather, he's told me, his family's been Viking; Gramps had Viking licence plates. B likes cold nights, northern lights, midnight sun; pillage and plunder where provided by law. His left eyebrow curls up wildly at the peak, a direct hand-me-down, he says, from Harald III Hardraade, the Norwegian king who was killed trying to conquer England in 1066, three weeks before the Battle of Hastings.

"Imagine," says B, "if old Harry'd made it. All those chip shops in the East End of London would be selling *lutefisk* now."

Harald also had one climbing eyebrow, B tells me with all the certainty of one who has a family photo tucked into his wallet to prove it. *Raade*, B explains, means "counsel." Harald gave hard counsel.

"You're saying he was frank?" It would be a trait they shared, along with the eyebrow.

"No, he was Harald. Frank and his brother Ralph came later." B's family also boasts a nineteenth-century sheep rustler who finished his career at the end of a noose. It's hard to tell whom he's prouder of, Harald or the poacher.

He's not proud of Norway's neighbours, the Swedes. Danes are fine – they used to be part of Norway, or vice versa. He's neutral on Finns, knows nothing much about them. But not Swedes. They might have settled a protectorate of their own, way back when with the other Vikings; they might have yawned roundly and put their feet up and stayed in a colony or two – if only they'd been energetic enough to get to it in the first place.

"The Swedish Vikings couldn't row?"

"Couldn't do anything, still can't." He's into his rhythm now, there's no stopping him. *On the row to Valhalla.* "They walked over to Russia now and then on a quiet day, just to stir things up. Otherwise they stayed home and did their hair. In braids."

B has had a poor opinion of the Swedes "since the war." At the outbreak of fighting, the Norwegians aligned with the Allies, and for their trouble were invaded by the Nazis and occupied for nearly six years. But Sweden declared itself neutral. Sheer laziness on their part, says B.

"How can you have hated them since the war? You weren't even around during the war."

"Some things keep."

Smike jumps into my lap. "Do you think the Vikings had cats?"

"Oh sure. They'd eat anything."

"Lots of Swedes can do lots of things," I say. "Ingmar Bergman. And Ingrid. ABBA. Björn Borg. You're telling me Björn Borg can't do anything?"

"Guy with the hair? Like I said, they do great hair."

"Okay. Whatever. Tell me about the radio stations."

"What radio stations? The Vikings didn't have radio stations. They just had drums."

"Come on," I protest. "The Vikings did not have drums. They weren't musical in the least."

"They weren't?" B looks chagrined. "You're saying I'm not musical?"

"You have a tin ear."

"I can play 'Whistle While You Work' on my armpit."

I'm well when B's around, but business calls him away for days on end. When he leaves Diamond for the first time, I'm felled by a migraine. Zelda's phone number rattles in my head. It's not even long distance now – if I had the strength I could go outside and yell to her across the fields – and yet we may as well be at opposite ends of the galaxy. It's eerie not to call her. Normally she'd be here, pottering around below while I lay down upstairs. I'd hear the kettle whistle. She'd bring me a cloth now and then. Maybe she'd tell me to lie on my ear, and I wouldn't mind a bit.

Carol's bedridden, incommunicado; I can't call her. What could I say, anyway? *I've got a migraine; how's your dying going?*

For the next four days, I creep around in a haze of painkillers, with a do-list in my head exacting as a recipe: *Open washer lid. Open dryer door. Transfer laundry. Pull out tights, drape over left shoulder. Close dryer door; turn dial to "More Dry"; set timer; press start. Hang tights over shower curtain rod on way out of bathroom. Check woodstove on way to kitchen. Continue on to kitchen. Take spring water out of fridge. Set on counter, fill kettle, cross room with kettle and plug it in. Listen for dryer timer. When timer sounds, return to bathroom. Open dryer door; pull out flannelettes, slightly damp; drape over left shoulder. Close dryer door; press start again for clothes remaining. Hang flannelettes over shower curtain rod next to tights, on way out of bathroom. Check woodstove on way back to kitchen.*

It's as if I don't have an ounce of wherewithal for backtracking or error. My movements are laid out like feet on the floor from Arthur Murray's Dance Studio.

Ask anyone who's routinely taken Tylenol 3. Codeine, like all the opioids, brings life down to a checklist whose exhaustive, ornamented detail is not only tolerable but entirely agreeable. Because the patient feels lucid, even euphoric, at having the events of the next minute (and then the next and the next) laid out in front of her, with no thought or effort on her part, she's well-disposed to the mundane. Particularly something mundane with many steps to it; say, housework. Codeine is a great drug to clean by.

So's pot. When I shared rooms with flatmates in university, two of us used to buy the others a joint a week in order to get the place picked up and vacuumed.

But codeine can make me sick, and I swim on Demerol instead, until it runs out. I've been parsing my Gravol, having discovered the blister pack in the bathroom nearly empty. B's been taking it at bedtime, I guess, as a Victorian would a nightly draught of laudanum. He likes simple fixes for problems I'd stew over and treat with a sledgehammer – if I could find it, if it hadn't gone the way of *The Valley of the Dolls*, for insomnia I'd be taking Seconal. B's different, uncomplicated. Of all the gifts I've given him, the roll of duct tape he got in his stocking last Christmas is what he's liked the best.

I down the last Gravol, wait a few minutes, then chase it with two Tylenol 3. I cross my fingers, hardly dare breathe lest it set off my stomach.

Now and then through these migraine days I sink in front of the TV. Dan Rather's doing the news, Karen McInnis the weather. Karen wears a fitted houndstooth jacket with slash pockets. The jacket is sleek, the sort of bandbox item Nancy Drew's friend Bess would wear, and it sets off her blonde shag. Both Dan and Karen – that's how I think of them, neighbours in for a drink – sport a tidy, blown-dry look, promise of a rightness, I think, of a heft in the world. On the Arts & Entertainment channel, Angel Clare is romancing Tess of the D'Urbervilles, who'll be dead in two hours and better off for it. *Knots Landing* is in rerun; Abby's kissing Gary Ewing in early days, before they break up and stalk and betray each other through the next seven seasons till the show is cancelled.

A kiss, a jacket, a neighbourly drink, the bonds we forge. The rightness of the world, heartache and release, the tides and the television seasons, celestial harmony . . . I feel the bounty of my life land on my skin like dew. I stroke the cat.

God, am I stoned.

At night, I dream that Carol is a best-selling novelist. Celebrated worldwide, she has several books in the stores. I'm reading the opening lines of her new one: *So you want to explode yourself. Follow these simple instructions* . . . For some reason, I find the words cogent, even stirring, the writing spare and lyrical. Enthusiastically, I leaf through the first chapter. The characters are fully fleshed. The cadence of the writing runs off the pages like notes from a harp.

What a talent. So where's she been hiding this all my life? *What else don't I know?* I turn to the last page. *You're welcome to write about this*, it says.

You're welcome to, you're welcome –

In medieval times, supplicants carried words around their necks as charms, believing they conveyed on the bearer what they described. *HOPE. TRUTH. PRECISION.*

Precision? Yes, precision. I've got to get this right. No matter that everyone sees how it ends. Just because of that, it's even more important I get it right. A stranger walks into a bar. A group of locals are sitting around a table, downing shots, calling out numbers, erupting into fits of laughter. That's all it takes to make them laugh: one of the group calls out a number – *sixteen! four! fifty-two!* – and the others roar, clutch their sides, fall from their chairs onto the floor. The newcomer is puzzled.

"What gives?" he asks.

"They're telling jokes," the barkeep says. "They've told the actual jokes so often they don't need to tell them any more. Every joke has a number now, and they just call out the numbers."

"I can do that," says the newcomer. He walks over to the table. "Twenty-nine!"

No one laughs.

"Well?" the newcomer asks, bewildered.

A grizzled local glares at him from the table. "You didn't tell it right," he says.

·～

I wake. B's not on his pillow. It comes to me: *still away.* The fire's gone out overnight. It's Day Five of my migraine. I place a hand on either cheek, gingerly turn my head back and forth. Nothing. I sit up in bed, lean down for my slippers. I snap my head back, flop it down again. Still nothing.

Downstairs, I twist up spills of yesterday's *Report on Business* for the fire, hang my head nearly upside down to set the kindling. Still nothing – there's no more pain in me anywhere.

It's over. I'm not euphoric, exactly – that comes with the prodrome the night before the migraine, a kind of sick cosmic joke. Afterward, I'm just relieved.

I sit quiet, grateful. I've come back from a trip, pulled up a chair, set down my bags. They were heavy, the walk was all uphill, and I don't need to tell anyone where I've been.

When B returns, I tuck into him at night. He's already asleep when I stroke his flank, curl my wrist round his hip and his abdomen, nestle my cheek against his back, between his shoulder blades. I listen, try not to breathe in order to hear whatever's there. I'm listening for anything growing – microscopic still, but uncontrolled. I'm listening so that I can shut it up, stamp it out while there's still time.

⌇

This is what a death sentence looks like:

DIAGNOSTIC IMAGING
Central Regional Health Board

CHIEF OF DIAGNOSTIC IMAGING
DON C — BSc., M.D., FRCPC

ABDOMINAL (U/S)

There are multiple hyper-echoic lesions throughout the hepatic parenchyma. In view of her history of colon carcinoma, these most likely represent metastasis.

There is a 1.9 cm. diameter stone in the lumen of the gallbladder. The gallbladder wall is neither thickened nor tender. The diameter of the common bile duct is normal.

The spleen, pancreas, kidneys, and aorta have unremarkable features.

There are no signs of adenopathy or ascites.

Don C — MD
DC/js

And this:

Queen Elizabeth II
Health Sciences Centre

Department of Pathology and Laboratory Medicine

ENDOCRINOLOGY

COLLECTION DATE: 99SEP16
COLLECTION TIME: 1130

PROCEDURE:	UNITS:	REF RANGE:
TUMOUR MARKERS		
CEA	ug/L	290.0

Immulite CEA Reference Range: March 1, 1999
Non-Smokers = less than 5.0 ug/L
Smokers = less than 10.0 ug/L

She asks me to write to the College of Physicians and Surgeons about her case. She gives me the last five years of her medical history from which to extract the facts. It shows me a Carol I didn't always know but might have guessed: a middle-aged woman concerned about a slow thyroid, high cholesterol, lumpy breasts, stiff joints, daily headaches, changing moles, thinning hair, thinning bones, peeling nails, inhalant allergies. Specialists' reports back to Carol's family doctor deem her sane enough, though not uncomplicated. They call her "chatty," "determined," "pleasant," "anxious." She's a G2, P2 (two pregnancies, two live births). She had a partial thyroidectomy in the 1980s, had a chunk of a breast removed before that, and an emergency hysterectomy a few years ago. I remember that one: she ran her office from her hospital bed nearly as soon as she was out from under anaesthetic. It was one of the things that brought us together – overwork, over which we were overly-responsible.

Since the hysterectomy, she's been careful about her health: was persistent with doctors, did regular breast self-exams, walked the dog three miles round the lake every morning. She ate the highest fibre diet I'd ever seen. Dinner at Carol's got you three-bean salad somehow worked into the dessert course. She always dressed for dinner, her own or anyone's. Bess, meet Nancy: she always had that bandbox look. When she threw over her arduous job, finally, for a little peace and quiet and freedom, she came to dinner at my house sporting her new look – leggings, a long, cabled sweater, and short black boots with ankle straps. She was chic. How determined she was, how precise about everything! *If a job's worth doing, it's worth doing well. Nancy's pulses* (she has more than one) *quicken when she smells a mystery, and she flushes with pleasure.*

She has a family history of heart disease on her mother's side worse than mine on my father's. Her mother, Helen, had died of a heart attack three years before, early on a Saturday morning. Her father, Bill, gave Carol's answering machine the news, Carol being out at the grocery store at the time. The information was time-sensitive, Bill believed. He was nothing if not efficient.

Bill had his own bout of bowel cancer shortly after Helen's death, but survived it and went forward with a colostomy.

Better he'd died, from Carol's point of view. What her father went forward to was a disaster for her. He took up again with his English first cousin, Eileen, with whom he'd had a romance in his youth. They married and he moved to England to join her, taking with him the American car, the black plastic composter, and the garden wheelbarrow, but not the photograph albums of the grand-children, Carol's kids. I can only take so much, Bill told Carol.

E-mails from father to daughter are signed *Eileen and Bill*, the names always in that order. Carol's e-mails back begin *Dear Father*. She's stopped e-mailing since she got sick, except for a short burst of messages that all say the same thing: *Stay the hell away.*

In life, Carol's mother was brittle, distant, disappointed. In death, she took on a sheen. She'd been beaten down by Bill. She lived with him all those years, after all, and look at the rat he turned out to be. In Carol's mind, her mother was rehabilitated.

To the College of Physicians and Surgeons:

Re: Complaint against B.D. O —, MD

On September 15th I was diagnosed by colonoscopy and biopsy with Stage IV adenocarcinoma of the sigmoid colon. An abdominal ultrasound the next day showed multiple sites of metastasis into my liver, and I was given a few months to live. My condition has deteriorated rapidly and I have been in palliative care in hospital since the middle of October.

I believe that Dr. B.D. O —'s failure to provide me an accurate diagnosis as well as appropriate care and follow-up when he attended me two years ago for symptoms of possible colon cancer will be responsible for my premature death at age 55, and I request an investigation and appropriate action by the College with all possible haste, given my clinical condition and my prognosis.

Following is an account of the events that have led to my current condition.

Precisely two years ago, on referral from my family physician Dr. C —, Dr. O — evaluated me for rectal bleeding. He noted that "particularly of concern is that [my] father had carcinoma of the rectum found last year when he was age 76." His colonoscopy found no polyps or cancers. He concluded that I had diverticulitis.

Neither Dr. O — nor Dr. C — ordered ongoing screening or follow-up for me. Neither Dr. C — nor I thought any more of the matter. I had occasional bleeding thereafter, which I assumed was caused by diverticulitis.

This past May, 18 months after Dr. O —'s colonoscopy, more substantial bleeding resumed. This time, Dr. C — referred me to Dr. S —, who noted that given my family history "I think it is important that we make sure there is no polyposis or other pathology." His colonoscopy in September had the dreadful outcome I reported above.

It is by now well-documented that the incidence of colorectal cancer begins to rise at age 40, and peaks at age 60 to 75. My age alone, therefore, put me at some risk; because of this the American Cancer Society recommends a yearly check in those aged 50 or more even if they have no other risk factors.

My family history put me at further risk: 6% to 10% of patients with colorectal cancer have inherited an increased tendency to develop it. Experts agree that anyone having parents, siblings, or children with colorectal cancer is at increased risk and needs more intense surveillance.

Even my gender put me at some increased risk, since colon cancer is more common in women than men.

Adenocarcinoma of the colon grows slowly. Dr. S — told me that the kind of cancer I have takes at least 3 to 5 years to develop, and agreed "it was a good question" why nothing more than diverticulitis was noted by a colonoscopy done only 18 months before my bleeding resumed.

Most researchers agree that colon cancer takes at least 5 years to develop; others say 10, and some say as much as 20 to 30. Whoever is right, it is clear that early diagnosis depends on routine examination. I should have had more than routine follow-up, given my family history and given that I had symptoms which are hallmarks of the disease.

How could Dr. O — confidently rule out coexisting cancer when symptoms then presenting were found to be caused by a fully-advanced Stage IV carcinoma a mere 18 months later? Clearly, my cancer was well-established and growing two years ago and probably much earlier. I submit that the evidence was there, and he missed it. If he thought he had ruled out cancer for the time being, despite my risk factors and unexplained symptoms he took no appropriate steps to have me followed to prevent it in future.

Colon cancer under more ideal conditions than I have experienced it is one of the most survivable of cancers: the five-year survival rate for patients with early-stage disease is close to 100%. At 52%, even the overall survival rate, while not good, still allows one to beat the odds. Dr. O — has deprived me of any chance of that.

I look forward to your reply at your very earliest convenience, since my time is short.

⌣

Yours very truly, I sign it. The staple of the lawyer's letter, obsequious, disingenuous, smarty-pants. Ordinarily, I get by with a simple *Yours truly.* Now, I'm pulling out the stops. For Carol, I want an arsenal.

The College of Physicians and Surgeons has a brochure it sends to people at odds with their doctors. It describes the complaints process, lists possible outcomes. Like the rest of the world, the college no longer expects mere results; it girds its loins with outcomes.

Way back in the 1920s, George Orwell pronounced insincerity the great enemy of clear language. Orwell was a man who liked black and white. Here, he said, are a few of the pretensions we use to dress up simple statements and lend an air of scientific impartiality to biased judgments: *phenomenon, element, individual, objective, categorical, effective, virtual, basic, primary, promote, constitute, exhibit, exploit, utilize, eliminate, liquidate.* Perhaps there weren't a lot of *outcomes* in Orwell's day; otherwise he would surely have mentioned them. There are certainly a lot of outcomes now. It's only advertisers today who still promise us *results* – lasting hair colour, diapers and pantyliners and Ziploc bags that don't leak, a tire grip or anti-lock brakes that get you through that winter drive, and little Janey in her carseat. After all, the people who write TV commercials have an interest in speaking our language. Beyond TV, though, all is outcomes: we haven't done results for years.

Outcomes are something you don't really have a hand in. Results, you do. The only place outside TV you'll still find mention of results are in job ads and performance appraisals. There, the results you get are up to you, and you'd better be results-oriented. Don't screw up.

The outcomes the College of Physicians and Surgeons might get aren't up to them. They'll come on the wind, or they won't: they're an accident of God, they're science, they're what happens, them's the breaks.

Outcomes are always preferable to results when they're likely to be untoward, as are the outcomes the college lists as possible: it might reprimand the doctor, or make him brush up on his schooling – in both cases, *with his consent*. I read the brochure twice, twice more. There it is, *with his consent*. You can't make this stuff up.

I'm sick, writing the complaint. After she dies, her family will get a careful letter. *Dr. O — is so very sorry. We're all so very sorry. Neoplasms* (the College of Physicians and Surgeons won't just say cancer, since anyone can) *are so very tricky to diagnose. . . . We still don't understand the mechanics of. . . .* In medical circles, at cocktail parties, at conferences funded by Wyeth and Lilly, she'll be whispered about, my Carol: the one I knew with the careful clothes, the skirts with knife-pleats, the wry smile and the lambent eyes, the vast heart, the jet waves and the blooming cheeks. The one they knew as *that hysteric, that run-in O had. Died fast. Close call.*

B has a joke. I can't get it out of my head. Guy on a train, first-class ticket, finds himself overrun with bugs – in his berth, in the dining car, in the smoking car . . . Bugs for days. When he gets home he fires off an angry letter to the management. Forthwith, he gets their reply: *Dear sir*, it reads. *We are horrified to hear that there were bugs on our train. We can't imagine where they came from. We've never had bugs on our trains before. Please be assured that we have already taken every step necessary to ensure that this never happens again. We look forward to your continued patronage. Yours very truly . . .*

Satisfied, our man is about to toss the letter away when he notices a small strip of paper at the bottom of the envelope. He shakes it out.

Send this guy the bug letter, it reads.

She makes minor changes to the letter before it goes. I've pulled the colonoscopy and ultrasound dates out of my memory, and I've

been a day off with both. She corrects them. What does it matter?
I wonder. The College of Physicians and Surgeons is hardly going
to care whether it was the fifteenth or the . . .

It hits me. She's already counting the days. Parsing them, like
cigarettes or Gravol when you know you're running out.

[TWO]

Spiders and Flies

The spider exterminator is from Australia. He's never seen Ayres Rock.

"Never?" I'm incredulous.

"Well, have you seen the Rockies?" He's knows it's a bad analogy as soon as he's made it. We've just come from two years in Vancouver, after all, and he's hardly in the door before we've begun complaining about it. We'll tell anyone who'll listen. It's our riff. Soon it will be replaced by our riff about Diamond, so we make the most of Vancouver even as it's upstaged.

Spiderman doesn't know *Picnic at Hanging Rock*, the book or the movie, and he doesn't know *A Cry in the Dark*. *Mythical, the Rock is mythical, how could you not have noticed?* That's what I want to tell him. But he's no fan of Peter Weir or Meryl Streep. "It's just a rock," he says, standing in the open hatchback of his truck screwing nozzles, hauling out lengths of hose.

He emigrated to Canada because of *a woman*. That's how he says it, with more rancour than gratitude, so I'm surprised to see that a wedding ring still survives on his finger. I imagine Mrs. Spiderman in her kitchen, standing on a chair, Raid in hand. Is her house full of spiders? Is her home overrun with pests, while the man of the house does for someone else? That's the case with the carpenters around here. Our renovations inch ahead, but I don't complain so long as the houses of the local tradesmen stand shuddering in their birthday suits.

To anyone who'll listen, however, I complain about the spiders. "It's a farm, isn't it?" my sister says. "Don't they kind of go with the territory?" As if that makes it all right.

Spiderman tells us he's using something natural, pyrethrins. It's like Raid that sticks around, he says, even though it won't hurt us or the cats. He wants to reassure us. He doesn't realize that I'd be happy with Sarin nerve gas, the kind Saddam used on the Kurds, the kind the AUM Shinrikyo terrorists used in their attack on the Tokyo subway. He doesn't know how little I care what it is, as long as it works. The spiders that have infiltrated our century farmhouse are, as Woody Allen said in *Annie Hall*, the size of Buicks. They have legs like carpet tacks. I venture into my study only with my socks pulled up high over my pants, looking like Payne Stewart, the golfer who wore the kneesocks and the knickers. What will I do in warmer weather? Bare feet, straight from bed, are out of the question. No answering e-mail in the middle of a sleepless night. Not in this house.

Our spiders are everywhere. They roam far and wide. They never take a day off or an evening either, and stairs are no obstacle. Once, turning down our bed upstairs, I find one tucked in for the night on the pillow.

⸱〜

The largest spider in Britain is called the Cardinal spider, after Cardinal Wolsey's sojourn in Hampton Court. The females grow legs four and a half inches long. In Wolsey's time, they scuttled round the palace at night on their stilts, terrorizing His Holiness. Cardinal Wolsey: royal almoner, lord chancellor, mastermind of the Star Chamber, heart of the Court of Requests. Not pestilence, not plague, famine, conspiracy, beheading, not betrayal into the hands of Henry – none of these things fazed Cardinal Wolsey like spiders did. A masser of wealth second only to the King's, and Wolsey still couldn't shake his spiders.

From Germany and the Ukraine comes a folk legend of the Christmas spider. Once upon a time, a gentle mother was busy cleaning house for the most wonderful day of the year, the day on which the Christ child came to bless its every corner. Not a speck of dust was left. Even the spiders had been banished from their cozy nook in the ceiling. To avoid her broom and mop, they fled to the farthest corner of the attic.

Christmas Eve at last! The tree, decorated, waited for the children to see it.

But the spiders wanted to see it too, as well as catch a glimpse of the Christ child. Out of their attic they crept, down the stairs and across the floor to wait in the crack in the door jamb. The door opened. They scurried into the room. They had to see the tree up close; after the attic, their eyes weren't accustomed to the brightness of the room. Up and down the branches they scurried, over every needle and twig. They inspected every one of the glistening decorations. Wonderful, they agreed. It was a splendid tree.

But alas! Everywhere they'd travelled they'd left their webs, and
when the little Christ child came to bless the house he was dismayed. He loved the spiders – they were God's creatures too – but
he doubted the housewife would feel the same. So he touched the
webs, turning then to silver and gold! Ever since, we've hung tinsel
on our Christmas trees. It glimmers like webs.

·‿

The thing I notice about this story – the thing any arachnophobe
will notice immediately and everyone else will not – is its lack of
closure. *What happened to those spiders?* One minute we have
them surfing the tree, webs and all, and the next minute they've
dropped off the storyboard. The webs are there, silver, gold, plat-
inum, diamond-crusted, whatever. But no spiders.

I would have added a line: *And the spiders, finally satisfied of
the tree's radiance and their place at the right hand of God, crept
back into their attic. Where a December gale swept in an open
window and flash-froze them dead.*

For the arachnophobe, spider closure is everything. *Get him*, I
say to B when I find one in the house. *Make sure you get him.
Don't bother to go after him at all if you don't plan to get him.
No room for error. Better he's alive where we can see him than
maimed and lurking where we can't. Make sure you get him. Did
you get him?*

·‿

"Are you sure you're going to get them?" I'm wringing my hands.
I have a lot riding on this.

"Yup."

"All of them?" For me, defeating spiders is like cutting out cancer. You just can't be happy with thinking you got most of it.

"Yup." Spiderman's adjusting his face mask. He sounds like that other Aussie, Paul Hogan, and as laid-back. With all the gators and crocs these Down-Unders have to tame, with all those dingos and tarantulas to defeat, you'd think they'd be higher strung. I want him to be wired, fierce, type A, perfectionist. When it comes to his job, I want him to be a psycho. He pulls his mask down on his chin, eyes me. "Look. Missus. I've done hundreds of houses. Yours is just another one. It's just a house. They're just spiders."

Just a house? *It's mythical, the house is mythical, how could you not have noticed?*

Just spiders? Stop anyone on the street, anyone at all, and see who'll agree.

"Just about everyone," B shrugs. Like most non-arachnophobes, he underestimates our numbers out there. And he underestimates the numbers of spiders.

Here's a partial list: Araneus, Bird Eating, Black House, Black Widow, Brown Recluse, Comb-Footed, Daddy Longlegs, Flower, Huntsman, Jewelled, Jumping, Ladybird, Leaf-Curling, Mouse, Net-Casting, Orb Weaver, Spitting, St. Andrew's Cross, Stick, Tarantula, Tent, Trap Door, Triangular, Water, White-Tailed, Wolf.

Want to know why the Spitting Spider is called that? No, you don't.

Spider experts have identified thirty thousand kinds of spiders and think there may be more, as many as two or three times more. Dreadful, yes. But what troubles me most is that there are spider experts at all – experts like Paul Hillyard, a "spider specialist" for the Natural History Museum in London who maintains England's

"national collection of spiders." Paul Hillyard's the kind of ghoul
who publishes barbecued spider recipes in hardcover books, and
who knows the truth about Miss Muffet. There was one, really –
the impeccably named Patience Muffet, daughter of a seventeenth-
century cleric and scholar who loved spiders and studied them
avidly, grating and stirring them and their webs into home reme-
dies with which he dosed poor Patience daily.

Spiders have been around. Fossilized spiders have been found
embedded in pieces of red sandstone nearly four hundred million
years old, from the Devonian period, and are known to have lived
in the Carboniferous period of Europe and America about three
hundred million years ago. Oligocene amber, from about thirty
million years ago, is full of spiders. They're more persistent than
some viruses. They can amputate their own legs; new ones appear
at the next moult. Some, like the jumping spider, can vault forty
times their length. They can live anywhere they can find food:
fields, woods, swamps, caves, deserts. Farmhouses. One kind of
spider spends most of its life underwater. Another kind lives near
the top of Mount Everest. Imagine, hoofing it all that way just to
run smack into a spider.

Here's the good news: the lifespan of arachnids in temperate
climes is a single season. Here's the bad: they perpetuate the
species from year to year, with eggs. In warm regions, some types
live longer. Tarantulas in captivity have survived for as long as
twenty years.

So, they've had long, rich lives. What I want to know is what
they're still doing in my house, along with the flies.

.◞

Cluster flies. *Pollenia rudis (Fabricius)*. Large, bumbling flies that invade homes to camp out raucously, straight through the winter and well into the next spring. Oversized, dopey-looking houseflies. Some people call them Window Sill flies; others just think, *Gee what a lot of flies we've got all of a sudden, look how sun-drugged they are on the south windows*. These are the folks whom cluster flies like best, folks who don't know what they've got till it's gone. Sanity, for instance. Peace and quiet. Sleep.

But it doesn't take long to find out all about them. In the country, a brisk fall night is all you need, two if you're a slow learner. In the morning, after you've lain awake all night from the buzzing, you can recognize cluster flies by the company they keep – armies of other cluster flies. They hum in the middle octave, key of F – and I wouldn't care if they knew four-part harmony. With each new day, sleep-deprived and stupefied, I sweep and vacuum cluster-fly corpses by the hundreds, as well as live ones too slow to dodge even me. More suicidal than lemmings, cluster flies die nightly in impressive numbers, buzzing their way to oblivion. But cluster flies are also like the vampires in *Night of the Living Dead*. New recruits replace them in equally impressive numbers. In the winter, we never put the vacuum cleaner away. It lives with us, stretched out like a robot dog at the foot of the bed.

"I wouldn't vacuum," says Carol. She's become fixed on this truth: let someone else vacuum. Spend your own time vacuuming, and not only will no one thank you for it, one day you'll wake up, vacuum in hand, and find you've Hoovered your life away. It's true: we've all done it. I remember this, from a compilation of under-grad essay and exam bloopers we kept in the student lounge in grad school: *Hamlet stabbed Polonius while he was hoovering behind the arras*. Did the court at Elsinore have cluster flies?

Pollenia rudis gets its common name from its habit of forming compact clusters of hibernating flies, commonly in wall voids or attics. It's found in Europe, Canada, and the U.S., except in states bordering the Gulf of Mexico. It lives wherever its host earthworm, *Allolobophora rosea (Savigny)*, lives, which is just about anywhere there's well-drained sill-loam soil with grass cover.

Cluster flies lack the stripes of the ordinary housefly (*Musca domestica*), but they're graced with golden thorax hairs your average housefly isn't. Their wingtips overlap at rest. You can imagine them, tanned, wings crossed pertly, stepped out of a bandbox and straight into a model's photo shoot. They're poised, natural blonds, and perfumy – they smell like buckwheat honey when they're crushed, and they leave a greasy spot. B can attest to that.

Adults overwinter in sheltered places, but they don't mate or multiply there. They emerge in the spring to mate, laying eggs in soil cracks. Larvae hatch in about three days, hitching onto worms. They become flies in about a month. There are usually four generations a year. In the fall again, as the days shorten and cool, cluster flies infiltrate buildings to hibernate. Typically they pick the same building year after year, sometimes travelling more than a mile to get there.

I learn all this from Spiderman, who's noticed our fly collection swarming the south, sun-warmed exterior wall of the house as soon as he steps from his truck. He's too concerned about flies for my liking, not enough about spiders. Cluster flies break into your house in volume in the fall, he says, through cracks around loose screens, in siding, along eaves. I imagine the cluster fly *Attack!* season, the scouting parties on the recon for a home as the frosts threaten, calling every cluster fly around once they've found one. I imagine them in their long rescue lines stretching that mile from the sill-loam soil to our house, slapping themselves to keep warm, passing their swaddled cluster-fly infants hand over hand to get them to safety first.

Once inside, cluster flies search out darkness, in wall voids and attics, for example, where they congregate in hordes. And map out a plan for how to keep the owners awake all night long.

B, too, leans a little too far in Spiderman's direction for my liking. He won't call a spider's web a web – instead, it's an engineering feat of a "single filament." He, too, thinks that at Diamond we have a problem with cluster flies, not with spiders. Some nights, at four in the morning, I can see his point. Once in the house, once they've overnighted a week or so in your dark attic, cluster flies warm up and look for light. The scouting party again: *C'mon, boys, the beach!* A Robert Duvall-type cluster fly at their head, in fatigues, fingering his Gatling gun: *I love the smell of napalm in the morning. Charlie don't surf!*

And so our cluster flies congregate on warm windowsills, on the backs of picture frames nestled cozily against interior walls, inside the shades of ceiling fixtures and bedside lamps – even bedside lamps that were extinguished hours before, when their owners turned in. Cluster flies have light memory. They migrate to living areas of the house through window casings and wall openings. And then they *buzz buzz buzz* all night long. Our house has become a playland for the noisiest, most populous flies you've ever seen.

But as there is not with the spiders, there is an upside to our flies. We have flies in spades. But we also have wall voids, floor voids. Without the flies, I'd never have known about the voids. I'm fascinated. *Void. A Star Trek* kind of word, full of darkness and possibility.

B is not fascinated that we have voids. He doesn't care in the least. He's fixed only on the flies that lurk in them, slumbering away till their own Brigadoon dawns at the touch of a thermostat, the switch of a light; just biding their time till they're up and at 'em and into the vacuum cleaner.

Think of the Borrowers, I say, those magical mini-folk living under a kitchen floorboard in Mary Norton's kid's books. Look what Mary Norton did with a void. Think of the possibilities for our voids, I say.

"I'm going out to feed the ducks," he says.

In *Zen and the Art of Motorcycle Maintenance*, Robert Pirsig writes about two kinds of mind. The classicist wants to know what's behind the curtain, and the romantic wants the classicist to notice that the curtain is beautiful. B, an engineer, doesn't even see the curtain as he snaps it back. "Unless you know something I don't" – it's his favourite saying.

"I don't know anything you don't," I like to say, "and quite a lot less."

Try it for yourself. Tell my B the story of Brigadoon. Tell him about Fiona and Tommy Albright, about the romance and the sorrow and enchantment. Mention the tears, the lovers torn from one another's arms, the witches, even. Mention fighting the fight. Don't forget to mention Mr. Lundie, and the miracles.

When you tell him how the place rouses itself every hundred years, make the romantic's nod in his classicist's direction by showing him you've done the math. "Every hundred years – that's every 36,500 days," tell him brightly.

"Uh huh," he'll say. His forehead will crease, he'll pick up a pencil and tap it on his palm, then throw it down suddenly and reach for his calculator. He'll stop himself briefly, look up at you. "This Brigadoon thing. It's accuracy you're after?"

Don't hesitate. You wanted something evocative and deep, but forget all that for now: accuracy will do.

He'll be relieved. Visibly. He's back to his calculator now. It's an engineer's calculator, with *TAN*s and *SIN*s and *XEQ*s and at least three functions to each key. It has no *ON* or *OFF* buttons; activating it must require an algorithm or some arcane formula, some engineer's secret handshake. It's a Reverse Polish Notation calculator to boot. I thought he was having me on about that, but he wasn't. Googling RPN yields a depressing 130,000 hits, all about as readable as this one:

> In the 1920s, Jan Lukasiewicz developed a formal logic system which allowed mathematical expressions to be specified without parentheses by placing the operators before (prefix notation) or after (postfix notation) the operands. For example the (infix notation) expression
>
> $$(4 + 5) \times 6$$
>
> could be expressed in prefix notation as
>
> $$\times\ 6 + 4\ 5 \text{ or } \times\ +\ 4\ 5\ 6$$
>
> and could be expressed in postfix notation as
>
> $$4\ 5 + 6 \times \text{ or } 6\ 4\ 5 + \times$$
>
> Prefix notation also came to be known as Polish Notation in honour of Lukasiewicz. Hewlett Packard adjusted the postfix

notation for a calculator keyboard, added a stack to hold the
operands and functions to reorder the stack. HP dubbed the
result Reverse Polish Notation (RPN), also in honour of
Lukasiewicz.

However he works it, whatever it all means, B's fingers fly over
his RPN calculator in service of accuracy in Brigadoon. He looks
up. "Well, then, if it's accuracy you're after, it's not every 36,500
days. It's every 36,524. You take a normal year, 365 days, and multiply it by 100. But every fourth year is a leap year, which has 366
days. A leap year is defined as a year divisible by four. However,
if a year is also divisible by 100, then it is *not* a leap year. However
again, if a year is divisible by 400, then it *is* a leap year – but you
don't need to get into that. The important thing is that if you
apply those rules to Brigadoon, that means you have to add 24
days to 36,500."

Today, a two-inch-wide disc that looks like a coffee coaster lies in
a city parking lot, chattering away at a cluster of small satellites
called Argos that whirl around the planet at an altitude of eight
hundred kilometres, about the distance between New York City
and Toronto: *here I am here I am here I am*. Worse than that girl
fish, B would say, it never shuts up, but it's cheaper and smaller
than GPS, and the best is yet to come – soon he'll make a second
generation that's even better. It will be surreptitious, nearly invisible, talking to new Argos that will hitchhike on the back of GPS
satellites, freeloading, saving their own steam to track contraband
drug traffic, hijacked shipping containers, protected sea turtles. For

now, you phone Toulouse, in France, to find out how Argos reads your coaster; soon, you'll phone any number of places in North America. Better, closer, controllable. B's coaster will natter away for five years on a battery the size of a dime. That's one box, this chatty little coaster: he has another that blows things up in a desert or on a mountain when some guy off the coast pushes a button a day's sail away.

B has made all sorts of boxes, and thought of more. But some he's declined to make at all. Like the one that Kevin showed up with in prototype at B's office one morning, years ago. Kevin brought along a buddy in full jungle fatigues, and a generic business card reading, Tec-Support Int'l Corp. The card was thin, the paper cheap, and "Corp" shrunken against the rest, added perhaps in afterthought as proof of Kevin's heft. It advertised twenty-four-hour phone reception at a number that had been crossed out and re-inked twice. Tec-Support Corp, said Kevin, was in the business of providing armed escorts to whomever, especially in South Africa, and a police agency there wanted more of this – a little gadget about half the size of a cigarette package that he produced from a briefcase. Just another barbecue starter, with two prongs protruding from the end? Maybe, but this one can drop a cow, said Kevin. A cow or a man, you choose, said Jungle Boy, sniggering. When Kevin pushed a red trigger on the side, a blue arc snapped between the probes. Could B make more?

Next morning, RCMP Customs and Excise stopped in at B's to visit; Harold L — of CSIS did too. The Mounties were businesslike and to-the-point, but Harold was garrulous and sociable, even prescient. He knew, he said, that B would keep him informed.

B did. When Kevin called to make a return appointment, B called Harold.

Kevin never made it back to B's office. A few days later, an early-morning raid on a home nearby turned up quantities of explosives, weapons, and grenades. A few more days later, and Kevin's jungle boy was found floating in Marina Del Rey harbour, dead of a gunshot. Kevin himself caught a plane to Hong Kong. It refuelled in Honolulu. U.S. Marshals boarded there and took him off to Montana, where he was wanted on a weapons charge and jailed.

.﹒ᴗ

I've never asked B to make a barbecue starter. Perhaps that's my problem. Should I aim higher?

When the United States can't export its foreign policy by diplomatic means, it turns to outfits like International Telephone & Telegraph. ITT funded the overthrow of the Allende government in Chile, has buoyed up countless revolutions throughout the world, and generally works to destabilize international regimes unfriendly to American interests. You thought ITT ran hotels? When it bought the Sheraton hotel chain and opened the Harbor Island Sheraton in San Diego, Richard Nixon cut the ribbon. When John McCone retired after five years as director of the CIA, he was appointed to the ITT board, and continued as ITT's consultant to the CIA for at least another five years. When the U.S. government doesn't want to get its hands dirty, they call ITT. When ITT wants a photo op, they call the U.S. government. *The Sovereign State of ITT* – that's what Anthony Sampson titled his book about all of this, and he wasn't kidding.

B was dropped into the deep end of the covert electronics business in 1966 in the suburbs of Saigon. Fresh out of school and a

Canadian at that, he'd been recruited by two uniformed officers from the U.S. air force and turned over to ITT, where he spent the next five years on its payroll. In Saigon, he and a legion of other engineers and techs ensured that the intelligence-gathering apparatus that occupied the top two floors of the U.S. embassy on Le Duan Boulevard did not want for anything – anything at all.

It may be that my technical problems now aren't challenging enough to interest him. I live with an engineer whose expertise in the black art of wireless is of the highest order, sought out by EXXON, ITT, and the U.S. air force alike. He does things so classified that he has to file his fingerprints. *If any fingerprint is not recorded,* the fingerprint form says, *give reason. If amputated, deformed, or injured, give date.* I worry about that. Harold, Kevin, Jungle Boy, Marina Del Rey. The sovereign state of ITT. And now, Diamond. Will anyone break into Diamond in the middle of some night and cut off his thumbs, just because he's been too top secret? At Diamond, sometimes, engineered things are that clandestine. But in order to tune stations in on my little pink Radio Shack transistor in the bathroom, I have to wedge it between two hairspray cans.

"Ummm," B says dreamily, hardly glancing up from his keyboard. "There can be a couple of reasons that works. The cans – they're metallic? They'll act as parasitic radiators in an antenna array. Or, they just serve as parasitic tuning elements for the existing antenna in the radio."

Well, then. As long as it's that, and not something dreadful. "Why doesn't it just work on its own?"

"It should."

"It doesn't."

"It should."

Well, then. As long as it should.

Men aren't from Mars at all – they're from the moon. The last time I had my computer into the shop, the guys there said the same thing: "It's not supposed to do that."

"It did," I said.

"It shouldn't," they said.

B was solidly on their side. "It's not supposed to do that," he said.

"It did," I said.

"It shouldn't," he said.

We were in the middle of dinner when the guys at the shop phoned to say they were nearly finished. "Don't know what it was," they said. "It shouldn't have done that."

"It did," I said, and got up to do the dishes so that B could get in a little extracurricular reading on *Low Noise Amplifier Design*. I scrubbed the pots and pans from the stove. I wiped the counters. I wrote *milk, garbage bags* on the grocery list, since he would never think to.

•⤳

Spider silk is stronger than the same thickness of steel. Dragline silk, the threads spiders dangle from and use to frame up their webs, is the strongest animal stuff there is, three times stronger even than the Kevlar that lines bulletproof vests. A one-inch diameter "rope" of dragline, if it could be woven from millions of strands, could tailhook a jet landing on an aircraft carrier.

Only some spiders engineer single filament webs. Others, the hunters and jumpers, have sharp eyesight that allows them to go out for lunch rather than stay in, waiting for delivery. The web builders are quick studies. Baby spiders can make perfect webs shortly after hatching. Cave spiders, sneaky bastards, spin their webs just inside a cave entrance, where insects still roam. It was a cave spider that saved Mohammed, the story is told, when the prophet fled Mecca and hid in a cave from the Koreishites. At its mouth an acacia sprang up in full leaf to cover him, complete with a wood-pigeon that built an instant nest in the branches, and a spider that secured things with a web. Nothing's gone into that cave lately, the Koreishites agreed when they came upon it, and they went on their way.

The most elaborate webs, the kind you see on dewy mornings, are designed by several spider families working together. Although web construction is complicated, it's usually done in the last hour before dawn. When dinner stumbles into it, a web gets damaged, so spiders repeat their work a lot. No one knows how they keep from sticking to their own webs, or how, when they need to, they cut the threads that are otherwise so elastic. To make an orb web, a spider releases a line of silk to the breeze. Spiders count on the wind a lot. Is that why they love Diamond? Small spiders sail on their lines for long distances in the wind, and at staggering heights – into the troposphere, at twenty-five hundred feet or more. B launches radio waves into the troposphere all the time. What's up there that a spider might crash into? I ask, hopefully.

Bits of airplanes, he says. Not much else.

Too bad.

In making an orb web, the spider hopes that the far end of an airborne line will snag on something distant – a twig, a fence post – and so become a guywire for the rest of the web. If it doesn't, she can reel it back in, eat it, and spit out another. Once she has her guywire, she crosses it like a bridge, securing reinforcing line. She descends then from the centre to attach a vertical guywire to the ground or something on it – another twig, perhaps. A bed, a pillow. *Lay your sleeping head, my love.* The centre of the web is established when the spider climbs back up with another thread, securing it well past the bridge's midpoint. Here we have the first spoke; others follow. Then, working outwards from the centre, she lays down rings of dry silk. Working her way back in, she removes the dry stuff and replaces it with sticky silk. The silk dries out eventually, and must be replaced – a spider's work is never done.

Carol visits the farm only once, soon after we move in. There's no waylaying her till we've unpacked enough to find places to sit. "I can't wait," she says on the phone, and she doesn't mean it in the way most people would.

Months before, we made our plans to move from Vancouver. "I can hardly wait!" she said. Back then she did mean it in the way most people would, because back then she was like most people, expecting the future to turn up on the doorstep each morning along with the newspaper. "I can hardly wait," she said then, "to see our stuff back home where it belongs."

Our stuff. We'd found it together, chosen it, and moved it into my nearly empty house. Decided what should go where. All because when I left my first husband we couldn't decide who should get what – and ever-efficient, he simply waited till I'd left for work one day, then backed a truck up to the door and robbed the place. While the lawyers lawyered, I needed a place to sit, and Carol and I visited the antiques dealers of Nova Scotia's scenic south shore: Lunenburg, Mahone Bay, Chester, Hubbards. The small things we found we stuffed into my old Cressida: rugs, a plant stand, a huge earthenware fruit bowl painted and fired with gorgeous enamels, even a full-height fold-down desk. Larger things we had delivered. The pine sideboard, the weathered blue hutch from the 1800s, the harvest table and the handpainted mirror and the dishes – these were "our things."

When she visited us on the west coast, it was "to see how our things were managing out of their element." They weren't hip, they weren't steel or square or black, they weren't inset with smoked or bevelled glass, they weren't modern in the least. Every Saturday, the Vancouver *Sun* ran a thick "New Homes" section full of furniture ads. I never saw anything I liked, but I saw lots of articles on how to get your houseplants through a West Coast winter, what to do when your mattress mildews. (Throw it out.) I'd never heard of it before – a mattress mildewing inside from months of rain outside. No wonder we had to get out of there.

Our things, says Carol on her first and last visit to Diamond, running a hand down the harvest table. As a housewarming gift she's brought me two delicate, tiny porcelain pots and saucers of painted chintz, for mini-violets. I'm more than surprised that she still thinks of gifts or anything much at all. I'm surprised again on my birthday a few weeks later, when two leaves arrive in the mail, oxidized with copper to a metallic blue-green and pressed onto heavy card stock. *I bought these last summer at The Black Duck in Lunenburg, with a view to framing*, the card says. *I do hope you like them as much as I do.* The hand is shaky, but classic. Next to hers, even then, my own writing has always been a disgrace. She'd been in the hospital for some time by then, and would've had to have mailed it from there. The card is pretty; it has pastels of birds and flowers sketched on it. *To every thing there is a season*, it reads.

The leaves are Acer Negundo – box elder maple – and Ginkgo Biloba. Ginkgo, for memory.

For her visit to Diamond, she's brought my mother along. We're hardly unpacked: the walls are bare and most of our clothes are still not out of wardrobe boxes. "You've stacked things nicely," my mother says, referring to the cartons, because there is not much else to comment on and because she's subscribed all her life to Thumper's advice to Bambi: *If you can't say anything nice, don't say anything at all.*

They've arrived windblown. My mother has the seasick look of someone who's stopped but thinks she's still moving. It's Carol's trademark, driving fast. She lost her blue Dodge Shadow to a speed-induced collision, but out of it she got a smart new VW Golf, metallic green. The Golf went even faster than the Shadow, and she's collected four speeding tickets in it during the two years she's had it. Carol's been pulled over and ticketed for speeding on every one of the province's major highways. "Pffft," she'd say. "Why go slow when you can go fast?"

She liked to back up fast too. She was dextrous with a car, and wanted men, in particular, to know it. When they leave the farm after lunch, she roars backwards down all five hundred feet of our narrow, overgrown driveway, straight and unerring as a bullet. My mother is white-knuckled all the way home.

Who can run the race with death? asked Dr. Johnson. Carol's no marathoner, especially when she sees from the backstretch how things stand at the finish. She's sensible. She's not like me. I never walked out on even the worst of the movies we saw together, while she shifted in her seat. "I paid my money," I'd say. "I want to see how it ends."

·—

Burial grounds are wonderful in the country: ancient, decrepit, mossy. The inscriptions on the stones, having slipped by lichen and erosion nearly out of the world, seem like coded messages from the past. They're urgent, arcane, just out of reach. *WiwaR to WoduridaR*. Before darkness falls on Spider Day, we photograph a few. We pack Smike and Frankie like snarling bookends back to front in their cage and drive off, cats and cameras, for the five-hour tour of the countryside that Spiderman has recommended.

Someone's just been buried in the Poplar Hill Cemetery. A berth of flowers spreads the grave full-length like a motley, bunched-up coverlet. There are peach-coloured glads, feathery shasta daisies in yellow and white, a few funereal lilies and baby's breath, and enough patriotic red and white carnations wound in red florist's ribbon to make the whole arrangement look like it could stand to take a salute. The grave is shouldered by a heap of red earth. This is the fulsome clay of the east, clumped and darkening in the damp fall air. Against it the florist's blooms seem ripe, nearly garish, for all their vigour not real in the least. The grave is on the edge of the cemetery, bordered by a wire fence, and the cows on the far side ignore it. The sun is persistent in the late afternoon, in the wrong place from any angle of this grave, and I try several shots. I keep my toes back from the lip, as if something might grab me from its far side and pull me in. The cats languish in the car. Smike is out of the cage by now and hiding hatefully underfoot, frothing at the mouth. Frankie remains boxed on the back seat, lying on her side, mournful, unresponsive. A breeze blows. On the shoulder of a September evening, it's cold. The graceless peeper now, the inter-loper, the animal abuser even, I'm unwelcome, and I back away. B's behind me; I stumble into him. The two of us teeter on the edge of the pit, swaying in each other's arms like rookie dancers. We're ridiculous, apologetic.

> *We were, fair queen,*
> *Two lads that thought there was no more behind*
> *But such a day to-morrow as to-day,*
> *And to be boy eternal.*

The body at our feet is an old woman's. I suppose it is, at least, though I don't know why I do. In this place it might as readily be a farmer – *might as well be a farmer*, folks hereabouts will say – his heart burned out under the sun and the clouds, just burned out one day from worry and work and watching the sky some nights, the TV others. Or it might be a younger man whose liver has gone on London Dock or his lungs on Players Navy Cut, someone who worked shifts at the Michelin plant in Granton and in the off-season, for something to do, robbed camps up the Diamond River, a crowbar in one hand and a beer in the other. It might be a boy hit by a pickup, fully loaded and glossy like you see here in the county, where income rides. And because death does the two-step, it might, eventually, be the driver too. The driver's fully loaded like his truck, after all; he has a two-four in the back. Or it might be a family of three – the father, the son, the brother-in-law – back from the bootlegger's, where they've been for a Sunday afternoon scoff, coming home and missing the astonishing curve of the Meadowville Road. A teenager on his all-terrain quad, hit in the head with a beer bottle launched by another teenager, from his. The surviving kid won't know why he threw it: a girl in dispute, perhaps; something to do, more likely. A few years ago, two kids from the village nearby got liquored up one winter night and called a taxi. One was named Christopher; the other, a year older, was Fraser. It was January second. What had Chris and Fraser done two nights earlier, how had they celebrated to welcome in the new year? Where had they set out for that night? On a deserted stretch of highway they had the taxi driver, a father of two, pull over. The fifteen-year-old in the back seat hauled out a piece of wire he'd concealed in his sleeve; that was Chris. In front in the passenger seat, Fraser, the sixteen-year-old, pulled out a hammer. The boys dumped the body in the trunk. They drove to the home of the older boy's girlfriend, where they played pool and divided up their haul – $65 and a pack of cigarettes. No one knows why the taxi driver died like this. The boys themselves, Pictou County Raskolnikovs of existential privilege, have never said.

The actuaries rend their garments here, tear their hair, throw down their charts. The police and the lawyers and the judiciary do too. There's no telling about death in Diamond. It just drives, up and down the road.

Who *are* those people on the road – our road, any road? There's no one to visit down here, and still the pickups creep by, all hours, on low beams. We ask around. Turns out that it's a social event. Buddy picks up buddy, they drink and drive. They have to, because the wife won't let them sit and drink at home.

·ᴗ

There's no accounting for what we do when the alarm sounds. Chris's mother, Claudia, had left the family years before, running off to art school in New York City, where she started another. When Chris was charged, she was suddenly back, camping out in a tent for the summer months of the trial in one of Zelda's fields. She had her ten-year-old, from the new family, in tow. She wouldn't be in the way, she promised, but she wasn't leaving either, and soon she was up at the house for pee breaks and baths and talks at the kitchen table. She was strung tighter than a Stradivarius, and under all that weight the table shivered. It was a rickety table. Claudia was good with her hands; she was brilliant; she had energy to burn; and over the course of the summer she flipped the thing over and back, over and back, taking it apart and reassembling it while she talked into the night, every night.

—

When Carol hears the bell, she shops full out for a week. She returns things, that is: a new cast-iron pot she'd just bought, a shoulder bag, a jacket for someone's wedding later in the fall, a new lightweight vacuum cleaner. John will marry again; she's known him thirty years, and she knows that's what he'll do. She'll be replaced. Why shouldn't her replacement have to lug around the old Hoover, just as she had to all these years? She won't talk about it any more than that – not about the vacuum cleaner, not about her replacement. She returns most everything, but she does buy one thing, and plenty of it: nightgowns.

She won't talk about the nightgowns either. She'll only quote Oscar Wilde: *Always forgive your enemies. Nothing annoys them so much.*

"Is John your enemy, then?"

"No." She looks surprised.

"Then who?"

"Everyone." She looks down into her cup a long time. "Everything."

Her nightgowns are cotton, smart, and never girlish. They're practical, with short sleeves to accommodate the IVs she'll have, the injections, the Duragesic pain patches they will press onto her upper arms and chest. While they don't need to be durable, they are. Only the best: Carol would have it no other way. My mother sends the French nightgowns that she's been saving in a trunk all her life.

Can you stand three girls? Can you adopt me? Carol asks her.

I already have, my mother says.

In her nightgowns, bought and borrowed, Carol will look like she's stepped out of a bandbox – and then lain down to catch the last of her breath.

She's pell-mell for a week, and for the next, and by the end of the second week she's turfed out her entire house, a job that mushrooms from cleaning out her underwear drawer. Boxes choke the deck, waiting for the Goodwill. She's moved furniture to accommodate the kids, who'll eventually have to come home; she's made up beds. She cleans out the fridge, lists and dates everything in the deep-freeze. She gives away half her plants. The hardest to part with are her orchids. One, with a huge lemony slipper, she worked over for ten years before it bloomed. She gives it away first. It's said that G. Gordon Liddy, the Watergate burglar, held his palm over an open flame to develop his will. If she'd thought of it, Carol would've done that too.

She presses me for the date she'll visit. She's on a schedule; she visits. She brings me houseplants. She eats almost nothing. I make the sandwiches she likes, the salad, the deep-dish lattice-crust fruit pie; but nothing suits. After they've gone and I clean up, it takes everything I have in me that day to scrape her plate into the compost. I think about wrapping it up, freezing it. It feels like her last meal. I can't bear to part with it, and I do.

·~

I haven't understood about Poplar Hill till now. The locals call it "Popular Hill," and I've supposed they mean choice: *Hettie's picked out her plot, paid for it already. Better drainage on a hill, that's what makes it popular.* But I've got the name right for our second stop, the Willis Cemetery. All the same, when we get there it seems a mistake. Mr. Willis left his name to the cemetery and some money to the town of Millsville nearby. He'd been born there in the middle of the 1800s, but as a young man he moved to Montreal, taking up the sewing machine business as well as the selling of pianos and organs. When he turned his hand to making them rather than selling them, he made his fortune.

The Willis Cemetery may be his in name, but according to the markers, it belongs almost entirely to the Henrys and the Raes: *In Memory of MATTHEW son of John Henry Who departed this life Decr 26th 1859 Aged 26 years; In Memory of THOMAS RAE Who died on the 30 December 1833 Aged 75 Years Also MARY REID his Spouse Who died on the 27 April 1837 Aged 80 Years Likewise JEAN REID Who died on the 6 November 1822 Aged 69 Years Also ELIZABETH, Daughter of the above who died February 29, 1831 Aged 3 Months.*

The Henrys generally *departed this life*, the Raes just *died*, but all *Those who sleep in Jesus will God bring with Him.*

The Willis Cemetery has a guest book inside a box marked, appropriately enough for the location, VISITOR'S BOO . The box, guest book and all, is wrapped in a green plastic garbage bag and wired to the cemetery's wrought-iron gates. The book holds the autographs of tourists from as far and wide as Philadelphia, Wales, Cuba.

The locals don't seem to stop to sign the book, or perhaps they never come up here. Who can blame them? We've come several miles round the mountain, winding our way in first and second gear up through the potholes, past the patches of clear-cut, the streams running hillside, and even a kind of second-hand furniture depot consisting of an old stove and a battered, flowered sofa someone's flung from the mountain road into a gulley. Eventually, we come to a sign that says → 𝔚𝔦𝔩𝔩𝔦𝔰 ℭ𝔢𝔪𝔢𝔯𝔢𝔯𝔶. Will there be a matching one, → 𝔅𝔩𝔞𝔦𝔯 𝔚𝔦𝔱𝔠𝔥?

Poplar Hill is one of the few local graveyards still in use. The Willis Cemetery is abandoned. It's antique, fallen into disrepair and disregard. But someone has been up and about, replacing the old plain-lettered sign with something in Gothic script that the tourists might like better. We find the old sign thrown in the brush by the road, and B tosses it in the back seat with the cats.

It worries me, taking a sign home where it may not belong, especially a cemetery sign. There are stories told of tourists from the mainland bagging up Hawaiian lava rock in their carry-ons, taking it back home to their rock gardens in Lancaster, Pennsylvania, say, or Butte. You have to ask each piece of the lava rock its permission, apparently; it has to be willing to relocate, or bad things befall you. Everything goes wrong, your kids break their limbs, you lose your job, the washer overflows, the CD player keeps skipping on "Wichita Lineman" or that's the only song the radio will tune in. Claudia appears in your field with a tent and won't leave. In short, you rain energy-field havoc down on your head.

The parascience of psychometry promises similar disasters when things get out of place. Psychometry supposes that personal objects hold the energy signatures of their owners. Thus a psychometrizing psychic can read you by touching your watch, say, or your wallet, provided you've had it awhile. So be careful whose sweater you borrow on a cool night!

The best psychically conductive materials are thought to be metal, though. The old Willis Cemetery sign is rotting wood. Maybe we'll be all right with it planted in the garden next year, amidst the dahlias, but I worry about Carol's ring. She wants me to have it when she's gone. It's her wedding ring, as psychically conductive as you can get, and it was her mother's wedding ring before her. It does not, then, come from the best lineage, as far as happy marriages go or even happiness of any kind. Maybe I'll bury it in the garden, next to the Willis Cemetery sign, let the ghosts of each duke it out.

⌣

Back at home, she goes to a lawyer downtown, even though she gets sick on the way and runs off to heave in an alley. It's not good news, he tells her. He does malpractice cases, and likely not very many if what he says is an indication. Nineteen out of twenty cases brought before the courts are deemed to be without merit; one out of twenty is allowed to proceed. Not quite a quarter of these that get the green light are successful – either by judgment or by out-of-court settlement.

It's notoriously hard to make the burden of proof in a malpractice case. You have to prove that your doctor was negligent (not
just wrong, or sloppy, or overworked, or conservative in his inves-
tigations). You then have to prove that his negligence caused your
problem, rather than merely having contributed to it or having
happened simultaneously.

And then you have to prove you have damages.

What damages do you have if you're a middle-aged woman who
worked at home and is now dead?

A suit costs in the neighbourhood of $25,000: about $5,000 in
out-of-pocket expenses to prepare it; another $1,000 to start the
action; $1,000 each for the screening of witnesses and evidence,
for consulting experts, and for discovery; and $10,000 to $20,000
to go to trial. Awards are in the neighbourhood of $30,000 to
$100,000; less if you've died before the verdict, and less again if
you're a woman.

Things are better on the other side of the courtroom. The
Canadian Medical Protection Association has a $1.4-billion reserve
fund to protect its members from suits.

Carol's next-door neighbour is also a lawyer, general practice;
by the second Saturday after her diagnosis, he has her will signed
and sealed.

The following week, she goes into the hospital and drops out
of sight.

She's told that chemo and radiation will be of no use. She's uninterested in therapies, alternatives, hope, miracles, and rumours of
miracles. We all accede. Mightn't it be impolite to question fate,
to argue with God? Off we go, gently as sheep, into that good
night. I think of Stephen Leacock, who took his wife, Beatrix, to

the ends of the earth to cure her breast cancer, who consulted as many quacks and doctors, who went to as many healers as hospitals, all because he loved Beatrix and wouldn't let her go, not if he didn't have to. Trix died regardless, but at least her husband tried to save her. I love Carol, and I don't try to save her. None of us tries. It doesn't add up. A funny man goes to the ends of the earth for love while the rest of us – sourpusses, soreheads, depressives, cynics, Englishmen – do nothing. Instead, we respect her wish. She doesn't want to die, but it looks like she has to, and so she wants to die *well*.

It's something she particularly wants to pass on to her kids, the last thing she can. She's taught her kids, after all, to cope by numbering their days. *I'm an eight today* – that means *I'm terrific, all systems go*.

The beauty of Carol's numbering system is how readily it keeps bad days in perspective. So you've fallen below a five today. Think again. It's not that easy. You have to be rigorous. You're a four? A two? Prove it. Measure it against your list of indicators. You can't just lie down and die.

The day my ex robbed me, the day she raced over and found me returned from work, sitting on the wide pine floorboards of my newly vacant, resoundingly hollow dining room, in the midst of soil from the plants the cats had dug up, in the midst of odd teacups and sideplates and wineglasses that the cats had played floor hockey with all afternoon – that day, and only that day, I was allowed to be a three.

"Leave me alone, I'm a one," I cried, dragging lengths of philodendron in circles through the dirt as if I were a four-year-old set down on an old bedsheet with my finger paints. My ex hadn't wanted the plants, just the furniture they were on, and he'd plunked them down in their pots all over the floor. "I'm not even a one. I'm off the charts."

"You can be a three, that's it. I'm being generous."

Throughout her illness, she wouldn't have wanted to fall so low as a five. At first, she imagined that even at the end she'd be better than that, far better. She'd drift up, in fact, to an eight or a nine in the bosom of her family, in the fullness of time, in the unfolding of the mystery. Ripeness is all; she'd feel that and drift. Up, up, and away.

But instead she was off the charts, and she knew it, and she hated it.

Some people have a serenity gene, that's what I think. Some people have it, and some people don't. I hear a celebrated writer and producer of Channel 4 shows in Britain say that he has it. He blows off critics and bad reviews with an easy *up yours*. He's dying too – pancreatic cancer, which is much like the liver cancer that assails Carol now. *I've never had a moment's terror since they told me*, he says.

Maybe that's how a good death happens, or doesn't. Whatever's in your genes.

Some people have the serenity gene, and some people don't. Some people have other things instead: a red, red smile, eyes so black they'll drown you, an exactness, a sense of right and for getting it right, a taste for danger and for calling late at night *to make sure you're okay*, a love for what's lovable and not for what's not.

Carol doesn't have the serenity gene. She wants to die well, and to be seen to die well. And she's not. It's why I have the keys to the fortress. I'm the only one who can be let in to know the terrible truth.

⤙

There are many theories about luck. The Hope Diamond is said to be so unlucky that whoever touches it dies.

It's true enough – just as it's true that whoever *doesn't* touch it dies too. After it left the Hope family, the blue heart was bought by the American jeweller Cartier, who caught the eye of the society girl Evalyn Walsh McLean with it by telling her it was unlucky.

It was just the sort of ruse that would appeal to a girl like Evalyn. Hers was a rags-to-riches story that courts tragedy, or at least hubris. It was a story of infinitely good luck, at first, her father having made a gold strike and moved the family from the American midwest to Washington, D.C., where she and her finery caught the eye of Ned McLean, heir to the *Washington Post*.

For an engagement present, Ned had already been to Cartier's and bought Evalyn an enormous diamond called the Star of India. Now, the couple squandered their families' wedding settlements on the second stone, the Hope. What was unlucky for others would turn lucky for her, Evalyn reasoned, just because *she* was lucky. Still, she took no chances, or at least Ned took none, and Cartier included a refund clause in the sale: if tragedy struck and any family member died within six months, he would take the stone back for a full refund.

No one died, but still Evalyn held her breath. She had the stone blessed – or exorcised. On their way to the church for the purpose, a tremendous electrical storm blew up. Perhaps a lightning strike hit the church, perhaps it didn't, but the story is told that Evalyn's maid fainted in the chapel and had to be revived. The storm blew out as fast as it had blown in. When the party exited to the street, they met bright sunshine and calm.

Evalyn relaxed, had the stone reset as her fancy took her, and wore it everywhere. But soon enough, the Hope Diamond called in its markers.

Vincent, her first-born, is killed when he runs into the street and is hit by a car. Ned and Evalyn drown their sorrows in drink, then Evalyn takes up morphine. Ned's divorce papers come served in gift-wrap, like a Christmas present. The McLean family heads for bankruptcy, and Ned is put into a home. The *Post* is auctioned for $825,000, and Evalyn runs around the day of the sale offering prospective buyers the diamond in its stead. At nineteen, her daughter, also named Evalyn, marries her mother's fifty-seven-year-old ex-boyfriend. She is dead in five years, of a sleeping-draught overdose. Evalyn follows her shortly after, dead of pneumonia.

The jeweller Harry Winston bought the Walsh jewels in 1949 for half a million dollars. After Evalyn's death they left the Walsh estate on a weekend, and there was some doubt as to their safety till Monday, when the banks reopened. Evalyn's jewels, the Hope Diamond among them, stayed the weekend with J. Edgar Hoover. Perhaps he tried them out with a little black dress.

The Hope Diamond had one last hurrah. Harry Winston donated it to the Smithsonian, recognizing that the United States was without a tradition of royalty and crown jewels but should not, thereby, be deprived of display gems of its own. Incredibly, Winston mailed his donation to the museum – though he did buy $1 million worth of insurance for it. Within a year, the mailman who delivered the diamond had his leg crushed in a traffic accident, lost his wife, and had his house catch fire.

·~

There are many theories about what causes cancer. Too many, really. You just wish they'd seize upon the right one, get on with it. Boil up the appropriate cure on the stove, inject it into everyone as a prophylactic like they do on *Star Trek*. How hard can it be?

That's what my friend Nick says. She has a gifted son, who at age eight borrowed all my Beatles albums as well as my boxed set of Narnia books. I'd read them so much they were falling apart. He liked them too, especially the character Jadis, the Ice Queen, more as she appeared in *The Magician's Nephew* than in her reprise in *The Lion, the Witch, and the Wardrobe*. He liked the portals too – the yellow and green rings that got you to different places, different times when you put them on and stepped into pools in the Wood Between the Worlds. Yes, this child was a winner, with taste and brains both. Nick said that if he'd just apply himself evenings and weekends at his makeshift lab bench in the basement, eventually (he's about twenty-eight in her mind's eye when she sees him in Stockholm, picking up his Nobel), he'd discover the cure for cancer. How hard can it be?

Medical students report that they develop symptoms of the maladies they learn about, especially the awful ones. Suddenly a headache isn't a headache any more; it's an adenocarcinoma. When Carol gets sick, I develop aches, pains, bumps that weren't there the day before. The place where I've grazed my gum with my toothbrush won't seem to heal. Smike the cat, who never gets sick, suddenly languishes and won't eat; we rush him to the vet on a blustery Sunday night in September, breaking down on the way with a flat tire in a deluge of wind and rain.

The devastation was all one could have hoped. Portents creep. Overnight, we have all the makings of a cancerous end.

And we probably do. Cancer is cell damage, plain and simple, a hiccup in DNA. Cancer is a disease in which the state of your genes counts for a lot – perhaps it counts for everything. The environment – toxins, traffic, noise, McDonald's fries, the whole catastrophe – it stresses us all, and stresses all our genes, sometimes making them divide improperly. Cancer may be just a numbers game. We all have about fifty trillion cells. In an average lifetime, most of these will divide fifty times. By your seventieth birthday, you'll have hosted 2,500,000,000,000,000 cell divisions – the number of stars in ten thousand Milky Ways. Let's say that environmental stress causes you just one genetic hiccup per billion cell divisions. That sounds conservative enough, but it means that each of us will generate about two million hiccups in a lifetime. Two million cancer cells. So why aren't we all cancer-riddled?

We are. We're getting cancer, at least. It's just that we may not be getting sick. Still, I have damaged DNA in my body, B in his. Our neighbour Everett, pouring another shot of Canadian Club in the trailer down the road, has damaged DNA in his. In his liver, for instance.

So why aren't we sick? The difference between us and Carol, at least for now, could be that we've somehow corrected or contained our tiny genetic time bombs with good immune systems and other genetic safeguards: genes that manufacture cancer-killing "tumour necrosis factors," for instance; or genes that make tumour necrosis factor attractants, to boost their power; even genes that turn off the taps on a tumour's blood supply.

Watch out for anti-spider Sarin gas, though, and watch out especially for emotional stress. It may have a hand in shutting your
safeguards off. The stress of eternal vigilance, for example; height-
ened arousal. When you're always on your guard – against spiders,
for instance – the increased adrenaline and cortisol coursing
through you damps down your immune system. I've been on my
guard against spiders all my life, never more so than in this house.
The wood downstairs is knotty pine, and after I've seen my first
wolf spider, every one of those knots looks like another, its legs
gathered under it, ready to spring at my throat.

·∽

On Spider Day, we've been gone four hours, ten minutes by the
time we return with the cats and the cameras from our tour of the
countryside. We're nearly an hour short of the five hours that
Spiderman has recommended. By this time none of us really cares
what poison still hangs in the air: the cats hate sightseeing. We turn
the key in the lock. Spiderman has pushed out all our furniture
from our walls, and has not pushed any of it back. It's a happy
mess to return to, a sign that he's been thorough.

The morning after Spider Day, we find a small spider. Hale and
hearty, no doubt with perfect DNA, she spins a gossamer ladder of
single filaments on the riser of the last step to our bedroom, her
stairway to heaven.

·∽

Do but imagine a poor creature, under all the weakness and
infirmities of age, set like a fool in the middle of a room, with

a rabble of ten towns round about her house; then her legs tied cross, that all the weight of her body might rest upon her seat. By that means, after some hours, that the circulation of the blood would be much stopped, her sitting would be as painful as the wooden horse. Then she must continue in her pain four and twenty hours, without either sleep or meat, and since this was their ungodly way of trial, what wonder was it, if when they were weary of their lives, they confessed any tales that would please them, and many times they knew not what.

– Bishop Francis Hutchinson, *Historical Essay Concerning Witchcraft* (1720)

I visit her in the hospital. Though she sleeps constantly, she does so upright. Whenever I arrive, asleep or awake she's always sitting up in bed. That way, she can keep her liver from stretching in her abdomen. Eating, or not eating, has by now become a constant theme. She's eating almost nothing – everything tastes terrible and turns her stomach – and she's surrounded by people who want her to. Not her friends, though. She's shut herself away behind the door of her private room. There's always a note on the door: *No Visitors Today Please.* She's even had her calls blocked at the hospital switchboard. But I know the secret handshake; I get through.

She reads me notes mailed to her in care of the hospital from friends she hasn't let in. They're plaintive, perplexed. She reads me her responses: they're firm, right-minded. They give away nothing. She's told me, proudly, about phone calls she'd mastered while she was still at home, from people she knew well enough but to whom she talked and talked without mentioning her condition. Might it be time now, finally, for her to give up a little of herself, to hand out bits that people might hold on to? I suggest it gingerly. *We all need something to hold on to, Carol.* A few fragile bits, like slivers of glass. *These fragments have I shored against my ruins.* But she wonders if these people are her friends, anyway. She's torn between anger and pity – for herself, for them. Loathing for herself that it isn't true, that *in the midst of winter, I finally learned that there was in me an invincible summer.* That it never can be true, because someone has killed her with neglect, and she will never get over it.

I don't know what to say. I know I would do no better, be no more generous. I know I would do a whole lot worse. There's something I used to say that she liked: *We must proceed as if we can make a difference, even if we can't.* I don't say it much any more. I'm not saying it now.

I don't say much of anything at all, and still I have always been the one she called on. She has always been the one I called on. She needs me, so she's given me the keys. She's asked me to bring her some crème brûlée from the Italian Market, and to write to the College of Physicians and Surgeons about her case. Armed with a duty roster, I perk up. Her hair, I notice, is thinner than ever. Maybe next visit she'll let me bring a curling iron.

◦‿

The church next to the hospital advertises ORGANIST PARKING on one side of the main door, IMMACULATE CONCEPTION PARKING on the other.

In the patients' common room in the palliative care ward there's a table piled with jigsaw puzzles – games for the very old as well as the very young. On the wall, there's a breast cancer poster that says patients can be visited by a breast cancer survivor. I'm surprised to see it in palliative care. Hope springs eternal.

There are signs everywhere, so many signs that you'd think there'd be a direction to go with them, some indication of a route. But there is not. In the children's hospital, there are train tracks to follow, painted in primary colours on the floor: red for the lab, blue for outpatients, and so on. Green for X-ray: the kids like that. There are machines in X-ray that might be able to make them glow in the dark, glow green like Kryptonite. On some floors of the children's hospital there are brightly coloured clown feet to follow, or the pastel wakes of cartoon ships on blue, blue waves. Here, there is nothing. You make it up as you go, and the hospital is a place of drift.

Carol's doctor is here to fix all that. He has the map. He oversees an acute care facility, this building, where patients can stay only so long as they're being treated. Once Carol's drugs have been determined and tested on her, and once they've worked reasonably well for a while, her treatment is considered finished. There's one big sign here that no one posts: LEAVE. Years ago when he was working in the North, B flew a Twin Otter into Sach's Harbour, an outpost on an island in the Arctic Ocean. The airport was a one-room shack, managed by a disgruntled import from the city who had posted a sign for the natives: PISS OUTSIDE. Carol's hospital should be so candid.

Under his appreciable eyebrows, her doctor looks like Groucho Marx. It's unfortunate, we both think. He's an economizer, and that's unfortunate too: the hospital's hired him to get people out of acute care as soon as possible. A conflict of interest in the care of most patients on the palliative ward seems likely, but we try not to worry. In any case, there's enough to worry about, with our not being able to get her meds straight.

At home, she's kept all her pill bottles together by standing them up in a cookie tin. The bottles are taller than the tin and the cover won't fit on, but they stay where they are because they're jammed together, there are that many of them. For easy dispensing, she's marked the drug names on the white bottle caps with a black marker.

When she goes to the hospital, she's hardly through Admitting when she's relieved of her cookie tin. "You can have it back when we get you fixed up and you go home again," the nurses tell her. Going into hospital is like going to jail. Your watch and your wallet leave you at the door. They wait in a baggie for your release.

⁓

There's just a single use spiders seem to have, and it's a dubious one: drug-testing. Dope a spider and it'll spin a really weird web. The more toxic the substance the spider gets, the more quantifiably deformed her web. Benzedrine, the classic amphetamine that got many a freshman through an all-nighter; marijuana; chloral hydrate, a common sedative – all these produce some pretty interesting webs. Because webs resemble crystal lattices, toxicologists can use statistical crystallography – analyzing the number of completed cells, spokes, and other geometry in the web – to gauge how much it goes out of whack when its maker gets a hit of something. That way, they can quantify how toxic the hit was. Soon, spiders may tell us not only that most drugs are bad for us, but how bad.

Spiders do drugs by ingesting specially dosed flies. A hash web is just not quite right, a bit untidy – and abandoned midway, as if its maker went off for a snack, or a nap. A mescaline web, to the unpractised eye, looks not very different from a normal one, but an LSD web's a beauty. It's a profusion of perfectly balanced, elongated spokes, and it's stretched vertically and very thin, as if Calvin

Klein had sketched it. The high-dose caffeine net is a shocker, simply a mess. It's full of great gaping holes and tears. It looks as if a truck ran it down.

⤚

By now, she's on fourteen different drugs. Five are for her stomach alone: Zantac, Gravol, Zofran, Haldol, Maxeran. They read like a list of bit players from *The Lord of the Rings*. The Haldol makes her stare, and something else makes her pupils widen into pools. When we talk, I feel my every moment's being watched, evaluated. The reality is that she's taking in far less of the facts than she ever did, and far more of the truth.

Soon I get used to it, I don't worry so much. "To die for," I say of the glam pink nightgown from my mother's trunk.

"To die for," she says of the crème brûlée I've brought from the Italian Market.

The nursing staff wear floral smocks, making the place look for all the world like a beauty salon. It's an odd sight for me. As a child I used to clean my mother's nursing shoes with a plastic bottle of watery white polish and a well-whitened sponge. She had her caps sent out to a Chinese laundry for starching, and they'd return to us unfolded and unfastened, with long flaps that Sally Field could have used for lift in *The Flying Nun*. My mother was serious about nursing – it was a fight she could fight. The rest of the time, she felt as defenceless as anyone else. When we were little girls, she had a recurring nightmare that someone was hunting down my sister and me. She was forever looking for places to hide the children in her dreams, hidden compartments or long closets or deep forests with hollowed-out trees where no one would think

to look. Awake, especially these days, she is more confrontational,
less defensive, and more resigned. *In me, an invincible winter.* The
enemy will take you sooner or later, that's what my mother thinks.
How many people has she presented, an arm around the shoulders, at the front lines?

When she was in nursing training, my mother sat all night by a
man's bedside as he died. She asked the night supervisor for permission to stay with him at the end of her shift. He was a tubercu-
lar veteran back from the front in 1945, separated from his wife.
He was handsome, still young, and his children would have been
small. No one had brought them to see him. Other than a minister
who'd been visiting, the patient was alone. On his last day, as he
suffocated under the bleeding in his lungs and burned with thirst
from a final fever, he asked for a minister. But a winter storm blew
outside, and no one could travel to the san at the outskirts of the
city. In those days, sans were kept to the outskirts, and only their
bathrooms had heat since TB was thought to thrive in it. My
mother ended her shift and spoke to the night supervisor. She went
to the nurses' residence to get her winter coat, and returned to the
ward to sit by her patient. *We must proceed as if we can make a
difference, even if we think we can't.* She felt his desolation and
his dread; she held his hand and told him how she admired his
courage. She fed him ice chips off a teaspoon. "God love you," he
said, and he died.

Can you stand three girls? Carol asks my mother. *Can you
adopt me?*

Carol's nurses amble through the piles of boxes and trays and
charts that litter the corridor. Stools are strewn down the halls and
pulled up to the drug cupboards outside every patient's room, their

doors always open and no one in sight. I could have had my fill of morphine and syringes several times over.

·⌣

Carson Drew, Nancy's father, is her best advocate. He is a famous lawyer with the means to support her expensive lifestyle. He is tall and good-looking, with a sense of humour. He wears glasses and smokes cigars. He wants Nancy to help him with his cases. He is also a good tennis player.

Behind the door of her fortress, Carol's distraught. She's discovered that John's been e-mailing Eileen and Bill behind her back. He's told them she's camped out in hospital, asking for more and more sedation. He complains that she's sleeping her life away. But he does say she's lost a lot of weight, and she looks good now that she's trim.

Carol has lost forty pounds in two and a half months. *Stay the hell away*, she screams at them all, as if John can never understand and Eileen and Bill can hear her all the way to England.

So long as her problems remain tied to the world, to days of fours and twos, we fend off mention of the D-word. But for a minute, now, with the discovery of John's treason, she breaks ranks. "When I think," she says, "about whether I'll be up here," – she casts her eyes up – "or down there –" Her eyes go down, and stay. "And when."

She cries and cries. *Be here now*, I tell her. *Try and be here now*.

·⌣

Be here now. It's good advice for those of us who will never afford RRSPs, traded commodities, gold bullion, diamonds – all those things that will keep us safe, if not now, then in the future. All the things that will make us free.

Well, freedom's just another word for nothing left to lose. Marty told me that like he made it up, the day he knocked on my door that first year in Vancouver and asked to use my cordless phone to call his dealer – drugs, that is, not investments. That year, that February, was the last time I really noticed RRSPs, and even then it was tough to focus. Marty clones populated our neighbourhood, distracting us from the requisite tax shelter advertising. All through the night there'd be mufflerless Trans Ams idling for long hours curbside. There'd be the din of car radios, people yelling down from their apartment balconies: "Hey! I've got a kid here. You wanna play that thing somewhere else?" Then women screaming, mailboxes flung into the street.

Sometimes the women got flung too; sometimes the ambulances followed and sometimes the boyfriends, repentant. Often, we'd fall back to sleep on the wings of some plaintive petition. "Hey, I'm clean, baby, come home," some Romeo would inform the neighbourhood. "I've been clean for *days*."

Sometimes there were gunshots. Backfires, B said, and then he asked for a baseball bat for his birthday. You women who find your men so hard to buy for, go to Vancouver and choose your weapon.

Since it was Marty on my doorstep that day, and since it was the afternoon and I was all alone in the house without a bat, I didn't like to seem, well, unneighbourly. He stood in my doorway and sniffed. He came often after that, and he seemed to have a constant cold. Sometimes he'd just sit on my doorstep, sniffing, turning over song lyrics *sotto voce* in a flat drone, waiting for that guy on the other end of the phone to turn up. Marty might have had a cellphone, but in Vancouver even the drug dealers slummed it sometimes, couldn't always afford what they needed. Besides, Marty wanted my company – my doorstep, at least – as much as he wanted my phone.

It was all okay with me. Marty was dangerous, and I had no trouble trusting him. He held no surprises. He was exactly what he appeared to be.

Depending on danger is a tradition with me, another invincible winter. Thirty years ago when kids at the Bloody Creek swimming hole told my sister and me there was a dead man at the bottom, rotting away, that he had bloated, scabby arms long enough to reach up, grab our ankles, and pull us down, we trusted them too. We ran away screaming, we thought it that likely. We believed in dead men, corpses, ghosts, all purulent and rotting: they were bound to turn up anywhere, dripping and hungry. Our parents had separated when we were three and four, and my mother had moved us far away from anything we knew. Our father put our mother in hospital more than once, breaking a flashlight over her head; I must have seen that, even at three, and cowered. Our father had been wealthy, but we started again from nothing. Years later my mother still mourned the loss of six blueberry pies she'd left in her deepfreeze back home; she packed us up and left that quickly. She'd picked the berries herself. To this day I think of blueberries as something I can't have. Blueberry pie costs way too much on the menu, even if it's the same price as apple.

I was three and my sister was four, and loss was already tracking us. Apprehension set on us like a fine mist, and danger became reliable, a way of life.

Danger is just the kind of thing you can trust, and I rely on it now. I expect it.

Look at Carol.

It's the promise of safety we can't trust, and these days, especially at tax shelter time, it's pushed at us everywhere – just because we can't trust it, or anything; just because inside our gated communities, behind our deadbolts, and wrapped round our ticking genes we're all scared to death. On her trips to the malls for returns of jackets and purchases of nightgowns after her diagnosis, Carol notes all the ads for *forever*. *Forever Young* posters in the windows of the women's clothing stores, *Forever Flavour* in the coffee places. On the TV, when she's home, inventorying the deep-freeze and packing for the hospital: *Ford. For now. Forever.*

Calvin Klein wants to sell us *Eternity*; back then, Marty was more into Being Here Now. He was like most of Vancouver, like us that year in that alien place, still scrabbling for cash with our salaries coming in. Once at a Shopper's Drug Mart I saw a guy have his MasterCard refused for a pack of smokes and a bottle of Pepsi. The clerk was nice about it, as clerks always were out there – they saw that kind of thing a lot. That night I said to B that the place could be no more harmful to human life than if we were living in one those 1950s sci-fi movies where killer spores are attacking from outer space.

On TV that year, there was a guy in an RRSP commercial tossing and turning. It's February, it's that time again, and he's broke. He can't sleep. He and the cat get up early, go down to the kitchen, and fish the newspaper out of the blue box. They find the ad from the investment company, calculate what a loan will buy them in RRSPs, and what it will cost.

There are a lot of numbers in the sound track to this commercial

– rates, dates, percentages, payouts. Buying RRSP loans must be scientific, or should seem so. But to my ear, all the numbers blurred into the pulse of a headache. B would've done better with them; he could have run them on his Reverse Polish Notation calculator. But he didn't. He doesn't give a toss about RRSPs – they don't have amplitude and radiation patterns. Whatever the numbers were, though, they were okay with this guy in the commercial and the cat, and side-by-side they run back up the stairs to wake mom with the good news. They can do RRSPs again this year after all! They can borrow to save! They can beat the deadline! These mutual funds have they shored against their ruins.

When Carol gets sick, I remember all this. What I can't remember is the name of the investment company in the commercial.

Fidelity?

No.

Acuity? First Trust?

No, no.

Clarica? Integra? Meritas? Why do these firms' names read like the cast of *The Pilgrim's Progress*?

The company name is gone. It's melted, drifted off like so many things. Nothing much any longer seems to have the heft of Marty on my doorstep, or the mailbox in the street.

⤳

I haven't always had the keys to the fortress. After her escape into the hospital it takes her some weeks to sort herself out. Then, suddenly, she can see me.

I go loaded down with balloons. The florist wants to throw in his own *Get Well* balloon, the message inscribed on it with hearts and roses and little scrolls all round. He's got pomaded hair and tattoos, he's earnest and overheated. He's got that Italian way. He pulls me into the back of the shop behind the cash register, and we stand by the helium tank and argue.

There might still be room for hope that only an outsider can see, he says. Next to us, his assistant puts final touches on a funeral wreath.

No, I say, and I win. But he insists on throwing in two balloons of his own anyway, no charge, no message. They have flowers stencilled on them; he's stuck on flowery balloons. He takes pains with the ribbons and the way they're tied. He tiers the whole great bunch into a tower.

Bang! A balloon bursts on the helium tank at my elbow. I shriek and jump. He clucks over me, wrings his hands. He asks her name. His face wrinkles into a plaster saint's. I feel like I've happened in on an episode of *Highway to Heaven*.

The day goes on like that, charged with small mercies. In the car, B warns me that the hospital may stop my balloons at the door. In Alberta, where he lived for many years, it seems every little nice thing has been legislated against by years of rightist government. But no one stops me. People open doors for me, I'm that loaded down.

They're a good thing, these balloons. Carol has sent all her flowers home with John because their fragrance made her sick, and her room's empty. Even the paperwhites in their bowl of pebbles are gone. I tie my balloons to the footrail of her bed.

"No," she says, "farther back," and makes me move them twice before she's satisfied.

I'm thrilled. She's still her old perfectionist self.

·⸱

Folklore about bad spiders is overstated. The truth is, all spiders are bad. An Australian schoolboy writing on his school's spider Web site puts it best: *Did you know that in seven years if you get bitten by a wolf spider, you could have no arm left because the wound from its bite eats a centimetre of skin every month and there is* NO *medicine for the bite.* The Brazilian wandering spider holds the record as the most venomous spider in the world; for Brazilian wanderers, this is bad news. The venom of the black widow, a nerve toxin, causes severe abdominal pain in humans but is rarely fatal. Neither does the black widow routinely have her mate for lunch.

Male spiders of all types do, however, normally die shortly after mating. The female gets to stay around a little longer, until she's menopausal or empty-nested – until her last egg sac is produced, or until the kids are out on their own.

The males of the species can have endearing habits when it comes to love. The male web spider woos by plucking the strings of its web. When the female approaches, he pets her. When wolf spiders and jumping spiders see a female, they wave. Some wolf spiders get together and jam, tapping leaves loudly enough that they can be heard from some distance. Some male spiders immobilize the jaws of the female while they mate: *love first, talk later, snacks after I've gone.* A crab spider wraps his mate up in silk, but not so tightly that she can't get away. It's a good deal, and she stays. The European nursery web spider bundles up a fly and presents it to his mate. If he can't find a fly, he wraps a pebble.

·

There were no spiders in Vancouver. When Carol visited, she noticed it right away. "You must think you've died and gone to heaven," she said. "Even if our things are wrong for the place."

We were stuck in traffic, inching up Marine Drive past the university lands. At this rate, it would take us hours to get home, but the glass was half full that day, as it was any day we spent together. It wasn't raining. As we inched, we got to gaze down all the cross streets lined with cherry trees in full blossom. "Why aren't there any spiders?"

"Dunno. B says they're too smart to come here, unlike the rest of us."

⁓

The spider featured in many old potions for the cure of illnesses like gout, ague, whooping cough, and asthma. You could crush and eat one mixed with a piece of its web in the day's millet, as poor Patience Muffet was made to do, or you could wear a small muslin bag of live ones around your neck.

Spiders are thought over the course of history to have made all kinds of great saves. They saved Mohammed in his cave. Perhaps they saved the whole of Scotland too, by toughening up the resolve of its liberator, Robert the Bruce. Even Frederick the Great of Prussia was saved, calling for more hot chocolate when a spider fell from the ceiling into his cup. Hearing the call from the kitchen, Frederick's cook killed himself. He'd poisoned the King's cup, and when the King yelled, the cook thought he'd been discovered.

Today, spiders are still thought to bring goodness, particularly if one drops from the ceiling onto your face. If you find a spider mixed up in your clothes, you can expect to win the lottery, get a raise, hear that old Aunt Lettie died and left you something. There's even a small red type known as the money spider. If you see a spider spinning a web, you're due for a new suit, shoes, at least.

The good luck attached to spiders probably originated in the Middle Ages, when spiders and insects infested most homes. The spiders kept the other insects down, along with the transmission of diseases they carried. Consequently, they were much favoured. The death of a spider brings on rain. It's unlucky to kill one, as the saying goes: "If you want to live and thrive, let a spider run alive."

In summer, Carol's garden is spectacular. Year-round, her house is full of plants. She has not a green thumb but a golden one. Orchids, hibiscus, Cape Primrose, Blue Nile agapanthus, poinsettia, and Christmas cactus bloom throughout the year in her windows, and house their fill of spiders. Like most gardeners except me, Carol doesn't mind them. John has been away on a long-term project when she gets her news. When she picks him up at the airport, he brushes a tiny spider from her hair. It tumbles to her collar, then falls to the floor. There, it gathers itself up, and all its luck, and runs away.

[THREE]

Our Hunting Fathers

Nova Scotia has no Sunday shopping, a small victory for the religious right, and no Sunday hunting either. For walking, hunting season's the best season of the year, clean and crisp, and yet we're reduced to one day's outing a week. But it's an equally small victory for us too: without the Sabbath it would be guns and Godlessness seven days a week, and we'd have no walks at all. Sunday mornings dawn; we wrap up in mufflers. We've bought toques the colour of the neon orangeade they sell at the Aberdeen Mall and we pull them down round our ears. We take no chances.

Halifax Chronicle-Herald, Bible Hill – Deer hunters are on target to have a great season, says the government's top big game specialist, Tony Nette.

With the deer season half over, reports coming in from deer registration stations show the kill could be 25% higher than last year.

At Kennedy's Food Mart in Bible Hill, Kevin Kennedy said 157 deer kill have been registered so far this season, compared to 200 for all of last season.

The general season opened Oct. 29 and runs until Dec. 4, excluding Sundays.

Deer hunting is regulated under the provincial Wildlife Act. Officials keep tabs through about 200 registration stations across the province – mainly private agents at grocery and general stores or sporting goods stores and outfitters. Hunters are required to register their kill with information on where and when they bagged the deer, along with its size, approximate age and sex.

The simple explanation for the increased deer kill can be found in last year's mild winter, Mr. Nette said. While there's not a straight-line correlation between mild winters, increasing deer herds and a larger kill, there is a definite connection, he said.

The deer population in the province peaked in the mid-1980s at about 120,000 and had fallen to 42,000 by 1995. It has now restabilized at about 76,300, which is a good number.

A resident license costs $21 plus tax, while a non-resident license costs $100 plus tax. About 55,000 licenses were sold last year, including 8,000 with antlerless stamps. This year, 17,000 antlerless stamps were issued, but the actual number of licenses sold won't be known until the end of the season.

"Hunters who haven't been out yet are hearing in coffee shops about the deer kill being up this season," Mr. Nette said.

Taverns, he means. During the season there's not a hunter to be found in a coffee shop for miles around. For one thing, the coffee shops are all too full of Mounties. For another, during the season, double doubles from Tim Hortons are hardly the hunter's preferred brew. When we drive to town, we see truck tracks fishtailing in the snow all over the back roads. It used to be you'd take your horse or your old pickup, throw a lunch in the back, go off for the day and bag yourself a deer. Now you take your $40,000 pickup with a $10,000 quad all-terrain vehicle in the back, next to a forty-ouncer of London Dock and another of Canadian Club, and several flats of beer. You don't come back with a deer, and you don't come back with a liver.

October twenty-ninth, the beginning of six weeks of hunting season. The sheep look whiter in the fields as the day approaches, the deer tawnier. Were they always that wide-eyed?

Dogs, on the other hand, look downright wrong, and I'm suspicious. "That's not like any sheepdog I've ever seen," I say to B as we drive by a dog in a sheep field. "It's white. White like Wile E. Coyote after a visit to the Acme Grain & Flour Co."

Hunters like us. That is, they like our land, its forty-seven-acre perimeter of forest that slopes down into sixty of wide-open pasture. Deer like to come down those slopes, blink in the sudden sun, walk around in the open air and stretch their legs. Does saunter up to our apple trees and help themselves, standing nearly upright to get to the better branches. Diamond Farm's deer vistas are legendary hereabouts, and despite the NO HUNTING signs we've nailed up everywhere on tree trunks and fence posts, every day we find pickup trucks tucked into the mouths of the trails and logging paths that run off our road. They're new, shiny, fully loaded.

We leave notes under their windshield wipers, polite at first: *You probably don't realize this is our land you're parked on, and our woods you're in. You might have noticed some* NO HUNTING *signs on your way in. Thanks for observing them in future.*

We don't sign our names. After we leave the first few, we're edgy. Will a bullet sail through the front window just as we sit down to dinner, an *Oh Yeah?* chasing it through the broken glass? *Kevin, Jungle Boy, Marina Del Rey.* It doesn't feel a whole lot different than when I lived in Vancouver and ran a network of women's clinics. I worked behind bulletproof glass in an office girdled by protective legislation, a physical bubble zone of the sort that surrounded the women's hospitals and the Morgentaler clinics. In theory, at least, it kept out anti-choice protesters, photographers, even killers. Arming for assault was no alarmist fantasy on our part; it had happened in the States, and a Canadian doctor had even been shot a couple neighbourhoods over. In Vancouver, we had security experts school us in the science of greasy spots on mail, and how to head off anthrax letters, and eventually, behind my bulletproof glass, I felt odd, but safe. At night, though, our apartment windows seemed to promise something that wasn't good. Every evening on getting home, I'd walk from room to room pulling closed the ceiling-to-floor drapes. The Centre for Disease Control was directly across the street, next to the main hospital. It had large vents on its roof, clearly designed to exhaust something. Its fourth floor looked into our living room, and between the prospect of flying bullets and accidental contagion, the nights were long. All the same, nothing happened there.

Nothing happens here, either; no missile comes sailing through our windows. In no time at all we become bold. We nail up a new sign:

NO TRESPASSING
NO HUNTING
NO EXCUSES

Our hunting fathers told the story, Auden wrote,

> *Of the sadness of the creatures*
> *Pitied the limits and the lack*
> *Set in their finished features.*

Our neighbour, Everett Pearl, raised on Canadian Club and chain-saws and looking like he's not long out of animal skins himself, won't have read it. Everett comes to ask if he can hunt on our land. Back down the road in their rustbucket trailer, Mrs. Everett and the kids and all the Everett dogs wait for word from us. They're like something out of Walker Evans. Everett himself, looking like he's halfway through electroshock therapy, is like something out of Diane Arbus. When he visits us he brings a sidekick, but not into the house. The second guy languishes in the panel van waiting for word too. B listens. Having done a half-year tour of Vietnam in the late 1960s, B finds it easy to talk to guys like Everett, guys with guns. He hunted here all last year before we took up residence, Everett tells us proudly. *Waited damn near t'whole winter camped out in yer barn there wi' the door open, waitin' for a buck to walk by. Brung over a chair from home so's I could sit.*

Is it Everett's chair that this year has become a pawn in a war between two local landowners? People are forever squabbling about their woodlots here, coveting their neighbours'. Private woodlot ownership is big business. There's so much of it in the

Canadian east that the region hasn't been snared with the rest of the country in export duties to the U.S., which are charged on wood cut from Crown land. Here, money does grow on trees, even on two-inch thick nursery stock that barely gets planted before the clear-cut czars shear it down. But Everett doesn't own a lot, not even a single tree, and he doesn't have the wherewithal to squabble. Perhaps he doesn't even have his chair any more; perhaps that was his chair outside in the road, blocking everyone's path. It turned up square in the middle of the Diamond Road one day, an upholstered, floral affair from the 1950s with piped cushions and a skirt splotched orange and harvest gold on brown. Over the days, it moved from side to side, from crossroads to crossroads, *quid pro quo* and tit for tat, until finally it came to rest on the shoulder, amid the ruins of the old schoolhouse. B and I sat in it and took each other's pictures; for us it was nostalgia already. *The Case of the Missing Armchair*, that's how Carolyn Keene would style it for Nancy Drew, but Nancy wouldn't come here. Her pulses wouldn't quicken – not a single one of them – at the thought of the Diamond woods.

B and Everett don't talk about the chair. They talk hunting. The word's not good, and Everett doesn't take it well. He's half-lit; he rocks back and forth in his Ski-doo boots and grips the back of my mother's antique cane chair. Everett has a thing for chairs. He entreats, he cajoles. Now that we won't let him lurk behind our barn doors and pick off unsuspecting does and their fawns feeding at our apple trees, we'll be responsible for his kids going hungry.

Everett's front teeth are out. A few days later, so is the back window of his old Dodge panel van. He's probably kicked it out himself to have a clear shot. Now, all he has to do is drive up a logging trail and sit there with his feet up against the back seat, his rifle on his lap. If something wanders by within range, he won't even have to get up, and he won't have to bring another chair from home.

·

B has been every bizarre place in the world, seen it all. Can Diamond be anything new?

Air Mike, the Air Micronesia flight, leaves Honolulu at midnight, seven days a week. Continental Airlines operates it with one of the original 727s – short, stubby, and dented. The back third of the plane is for passengers, the front two-thirds for cargo: groceries and mail going to each of its stops. If you take Air Mike to its conclusion, packed in there just behind the lettuce and the milk, you get to Guam, but the first stop, 825 miles to the west, is Johnson Atoll. B's been there. Owned by the U.S. government, the atoll is bisected by a runway. Concrete bunkers line the strip on either side, brimming with chemicals considered surplus to the needs of the U.S. military. There are thirteen thousand land mines holding nerve gas, for example, and about three hundred thousand missiles full of Sarin and blister gas. There's probably not a spider for miles. Garrison staff carry antidotes in hypodermics and have orders to inject themselves at the first sign of a leak.

Next stop on Air Mike is Kwajalein Island, the bull's eye for the ICBM Pacific Missile Test Range. B's been there, watching long-range missiles launched a half-hour before from Vandenberg Air Force Base in California splash down a few miles away. Kwajalein holds secrets, or tries to, and passengers landing there on commercial flights are told to lower their window shades and refrain from taking pictures. Once they're on the ground, they gawk out at the mushroom-shaped radar antennas beside the runway that track the Vandenberg missiles, and the manicured golf course for the Kwajalein techs. They take pictures. No one gets shot.

Next, Kiribati, originally the Gilbert Islands and pronounced *kee-ree-bus*, the native voicing of "Gilberts." This is a republic whose capital, resting on an impossibly long spit of land, used to have the International Date Line running through it, so that one end of the place was perpetually a day ahead of the other. B's been there too, both days. The republic is a clot of islands totalling seven hundred square kilometres – about four times the size of Washington, D.C. – but it reaches farther, claiming sovereignty over three million more square kilometres of ocean, about the size of two Quebecs.

Finally, around noon the next day, comes Ponape, capital of the Federated States of Micronesia. B's been there too. Like Kiribati, Micronesia is also the size of four D.C.s, and controls its own two Quebecsful of ocean. It lays claim to the highest unemployment rate in the world – at more than 80 per cent, far higher even than the wilds of northern Nova Scotia's Pictou County, near Diamond. Micronesia's primary export is black pepper, and there's nothing to do there but sneeze. In Micronesia, you can long for home. To call there, you trudge uphill to the Intelsat station, where you deposit a wad of cash with the duty tech against the whopping long-distance charges you're going to incur. Micronesia is a lonely place, escape is all uphill, and you're not likely to meet anyone, coming or going.

Some days, B feels at home here at Diamond, next to nowhere as we are. Some days, the farm is as quiet as Ponape's Intelsat station – but not during hunting season, and not during year-round clear-cutting season when gravel trucks roar past us on their way to shore up the logging roads they're ruining, and when logging trucks screech back up with the spoils of the forest.

⤳

You can't hunt deer here without a licence, and to get one you have to be eighteen or older. If you fall a year or two short of eighteen, dad or big brother can get a licence for you, so long as they supervise you when you're out using it.

Where we live, the licencing process approaches rocket science. First, you have to have a valid Firearm Hunting Certificate – $75 after you take about six hours of instruction in safe firearms handling and another seven or eight hours in ecology and wildlife management, hunter ethics, laws and regs, field and survival skills. There's a written test with a pass mark of 80 per cent.

In addition to your Firearm Hunting Certificate, if you're found carrying a gun in any wildlife habitat, you could be asked to produce either a valid Firearms Acquisition Certificate, a Firearm Possession & Acquisition Licence, an Adult (Firearms) Possession Only Licence, or a Minor's (Firearms) Possession Only Licence.

Once you have your Firearm Hunting Certificate, you get what's called a Base Licence "for hunting and furharvesting." And then you buy a Deer Hunting Stamp and paste it on your base licence. Voilà, you have a Deer Hunting Licence. This costs you an additional $24 if you live here, $115 if you don't.

When you get your licence, you also get one or more tags. The number depends on what Tony Nette in the Big Game Office at Bible Hill has pronounced about the deer population that year. If you kill a deer, you attach one of your tags to it and deliver it to the nearest deer registration station, where you note its particulars on a Deer Registration Form. Once you've used up your tags, your season is closed.

If you kill a deer, a moose, or a rabbit, pheasant, or grouse, and want to store it in the deep-freeze for more than a couple months, you also need a Meat Permit (Wildlife): no charge. Just hang on to your Deer Hunting Stamp.

For the past several years here, armed with all your licences, you could go off to the woods with your six-pack and bag yourself a deer – but not just any deer. Back then, you were restricted to an antlered buck only, and only one of those. That changed recently, with mild winters and growth in the deer herd. Suddenly, antlerless deer became fair game too, though you had to scramble along with the next guy for your chance to play. You put your name into a draw for an antlerless deer licence, at 1-900-565-DEER, or www.deerdraw.ca. Six bucks, non-refundable. In the first year, six thousand hopefuls ponied up in the first four days of the draw, hoping to get a shot at a young buck or a doe.

At Bambi, that is, or Bambi's mom.

·⤳

Three bootleggers live nearby. During hunting season business is good, and the Mounties look the other way: after all, a few after-hours retail outlets can keep the moonshining down. For several weeks we're not sure if there's been anyone at all we've passed on the road who hasn't been drunk. Not just drinking; all-out drunk.

"And I'm not even sure about you half the time," B says to me from behind the wheel.

Pickups crawl up and down the Diamond Road, scoping the forest on either side. If you want to get to town, you have to pass the pageant of orange caps and vests by jumping in and out of your lane like a stock-car driver. On Saturday mornings, everyone's out on the road, and you have to drive in the oncoming lane almost all the way to the pavement of the 256.

One day at the end of road, just short of its intersection with real life and police patrols at the 256, we pass a car that's just pulled over at a dizzy angle and hiccupped to a stop. The driver lurches out. Perhaps he's looking for Everett's chair: he looks like he needs a rest. He's corpulent, red-faced, a cardiac event in the making, and he trips over his feet with such force that one of his Greb Kodiaks comes off and topples into a rut in the middle of the road. But he's intent on other things, winding himself round the front of the car by leaning over it and walking the bonnet with his hands. With great effort he sways to a standstill at the ditch on the far side of the car, unzips, and has a pee.

The guy in the passenger seat gets out of the car, walks round the back, and gets in again on the driver's side. He's a little less drunk than the first guy, and he'll take over now as they leave the back roads behind. When we pass he tips his orange ball cap to us. Knowingly, he holds up the boot he's retrieved on his circumnavigation of the car, as if it's some prize he's won that we all can share. The guy at the edge of the ditch turns to us too, and nods. It's a wonder he keeps his balance.

It's hard to imagine I ever worried about a grade school exam, or even a university final. Both these guys have studied fifteen hours and scored 80 per cent on Firearms Safety and Hunter Ed, they've figured out the licencing system, and they're still on their feet.

·~

They kept him awake several Nights together and ran him backwards and forwards about the Room, until he was out of Breath. Then they rested him a little, and then ran him again; and thus they did for several Days and Nights together, till he was weary of his life, and was scarce sensible of what he said or did.

    – C. L. Ewen, *Witchcraft in the Star Chamber*, 1938

Carol has been discharged by the Economizer, who won that battle on behalf of the hospital's operating budget. The palliative unit's brochure says it best: *Whenever possible, patients return to the community.* It's another of those George Orwell words, *community*, meaning nothing at all except when you need it to, to get your way. The Economizer's got his way, but not for long. She's sick, she's dying, she needs care, and so she's had to come back – and the control she had at home, briefly, over her drugs is gone once more. Once again, it's a constant three-way struggle: the patient, the nurses, the pills. I've tucked her cookie tin in a dresser drawer when we arrive back at the hospital, but it's no time at all before we're asked for it and have to give it up.

She depends on the hospital for pain relief, sleep, serenity; and they fail her every time. For her pain, a fentanyl drip would have worked better than the patch they have her on, but discharge is already again on their minds – this time, to a chronic care or a palliative facility. They can't get her out of here and into there if she's on an IV, so they use a patch. The nurses keep getting her meds mixed up, and dispense them late. Three of her pills keep her nausea down and her digestion working. These have to be taken before meals, but typically they arrive an hour after the kitchen staff have come and gone, and come again to retrieve her tray. And then there are the doctors, who decide she can't have backup sleeping pills to get her through bad nights. Nothing after 3 a.m. – she might oversleep and miss breakfast.

It's as if no one's noticed that she hasn't eaten for weeks, and that there's nothing to get up for any more.

I'm exhausted by her drugs. Since no one else can, we need to keep them straight, and to that end we've listed them several times, starting anew with a fresh sheet anytime there's a change of drug or dose or schedule:

Duragesic patch (for pain; it's changed every 72 hours)

Before breakfast
    1 Losec (for gastric reflux)
    1 Prepulsid (also for reflux)
    2 Decadron (a steroid; it depresses liver inflammation and nausea)

After breakfast
    1 mg. Nystatin (fungicide mouthwash; it prevents thrush)

Mid-morning
    1 Premarin (hormone replacement therapy for menopause)
    1 Zofran (for nausea)
    1–2 Ritalin (a stimulant, in adults)
    3 Dulcolax (a laxative)
    2 Senokot-S (a stool softener)

Before lunch

1 Losec
1 Prepulsid
2 Decadron

Before supper
1 Losec
1 Prepulsid

After supper
1 mg. Nystatin

1 hour before bedtime:
1 Nozinan (for sleep)

At bedtime:
2 Imovane (for sleep)
3 clonazepam (a tranquilizer)
2 Senokot-S
3 Dulcolax
1 Prepulsid
1 Zofran
1 mg. Nystatin

p.r.n.:
Dilaudid (for breakthrough pain)
clonazepam
Gravol

In the world of pharmacology, there are rescue meds and there are prophylactics, or preventatives. The drugs used to treat asthma

are a good example of the difference, and often an asthmatic uses
both. He has an inhaler for acute attacks, and that's a rescue med
– as is Aspirin, for example, when you take it to reduce a fever or
treat an ache. But the asthmatic may also have a steroid inhaler
that he uses regularly, to damp down bronchial inflammation and
prevent acute attacks. That's a prophylactic – as is Aspirin when
you're a middle-aged man taking half of one daily to keep your
platelets from sticking together, to reduce your risk of heart attack.

I go through the latest list. It seems to me she's not taking nearly
enough rescue meds. In principle, it bothers me. She's taking prophylactics to prevent nausea, bowel obstruction, thrush in her
mouth. Even sleeping pills, when they're allowed, to prevent consciousness when it's not wanted. But nothing to bring her back,
even briefly, to a happier time. *We want more rescue meds at this
bed*, I want to say, but I've been at this awhile and now I say
nothing at all.

•҈

In the summer, our nine ducks swim in their pond at the far end of
the south meadow, just under the lip of the Diamond Road. The
house and the duck barn are a ways away, separated from the pond
by a field of long grass. Like Moses parting the Red Sea, B mows a
strip between the pond and the barn that takes him nearly all day,
the grass is that long and the field that wide. What emerges is a
duck walk, and our ducks take to it, racing down it to the barn at
suppertime, using the grass on either side for cover.

Festus Duck is the lame duck, the one we name, the one we love.
He has a deformed foot and can't really walk. He especially can't
run, so he launches himself across the field behind the others,

hydrofoiling along the top of the long grass on wild wings. Festus is always bringing up the rear. When he crash-lands, he tumbles head over heels into the back of the line, like a basketball with feathers.

Funny ducks – you'd think I could line them all up when I need to. But duck walk or not, some evenings they won't mind, and they stay out on their pond by the road while we lie in bed listening to the coyotes go by.

Festus Duck goes missing at the height of hunting season. It's Sunday again, the one day of the week that hunters lay down their guns; for once it doesn't sound like the Tet Offensive outside. B and I set off in opposite directions around the duck pond in the south field by the road, kicking through the long grass where the flock sometimes likes to nest. There aren't any telltale feathers. It's hardly likely that even the hunters have bothered to bag him, not in deer season. We can't imagine where he's got to.

He's not to be found in the grass around the duck pond, dead or alive. "Never mind electronics engineering," I hear B call across the water. He holds up a beer bottle. "Here's what we can do for a living – turn in empties."

We walk up and down the duck walk. *We must proceed as if we can make a difference, even if – already – we think we can't.* We kick through the west field, the east field, the back forty. We kick over every bit of clearing we own. That's how search parties cover open land, looking for someone who's lost. Keeping about an arm's length apart, they kick their way methodically through the scrub and the long grass. Whoever it is that's lost, they figure he's no longer on his feet but long ago gone down.

In the countryside around Saigon thirty years ago, B saw Vietnamese soldiers carrying live ducks into battle, for eventual food. So long as they hung upside down with their feet tied together like knapsacks on the soldiers' backs, the ducks were quiet. But the troops worried about backpacking the birds into battle, especially into ambushes they were planning. What if they got alarmed, and gave the position away?

I walk the fields, listening – for a little quack, a sign, a position, anything at all from Festus. What's the good of a quiet duck here? A duck's quack can't even echo. And what's the good of a topsy duck, a nearly dead duck?

Festus was never on his feet to begin with. As we walk, my feet don't feel like they're under me either. Around me, something is sinking. *With a little patience, the heart of Diamond can be found.* I don't think so, never less than now. We're in foreign lands, and it's beginning to show. We're not going to be able to keep the things we'd like. The loggers, the hunters, the spiders, Claudia in her tent – all these stay; we can't shake them. But around what we want there's an essential entropy at work, a spinning away of what should stay. It's like the axiom of physics that sees everything move away from everything else, flying apart in some last hurrah of the Big Bang. Before we came to Diamond thirty or more ducks lived here, and Scarlet and Jo left them to fend for themselves. Professed animal lovers, the previous owners, they left their geese too. It's been hard for us to figure Scarlet and Jo; to us, they feel like foreigners too. The geese they abandoned are wild now, the few who survived, and you can still come across them beating through the bushes far up on the hill, in the scrub of the clear-cuts. Abandoned, the thirty ducks didn't take to the hills. Ducks are timid creatures. Scarlet and Jo's cast-offs hung out through the winter at the edge of the pond, waiting for an occasional thaw at its centre. Prisoners of hope, they huddled, starved; they didn't know what to do with themselves. Some of the locals brought rifles, and picked them off for sport.

They've been through a lot, these nine ducks that are left. Eight, now, with Festus gone.

We walk. Something is sinking in me too. *This is the way it's going to be. This is the way it's going to be*: it's a mantra that becomes a marching step. B's got his rubber boots on, the tall green galoshes with the sloppy laces that the locals call unemployment boots. Once they're laid off from Michelin or the Scott paper mill, men buy those boots with their first cheque: toad-green galoshes lined warm for winter, manila soles, gold ties. B bought his at Wal-Mart like everybody else, but still there's a magic to them. He puts them on to take the water bucket down to the brook for the ducks. After a cold night, he has to break the ice with his heel.

Did you? Did you break the ice? I ask him when he comes in these frosty mornings. We're in foreign lands.

I broke the ice. He says it like he's been at this forever, and only him, and he takes off his boots.

B walks the stream in his boots. I walk the bank beside him, in mine. It winds by the house, and we follow it all the way down to the dugout bordering on our woods. When we get to the dugout we walk its long perimeter in opposite directions, crossing at the back. Wild iris has grown here in spring, but everything is matted down now, preparing for ruin. As we pass, we don't say a word. We meet again at the top. B takes my hand. He threads his fingers through mine, squeezes hard. I look down, I keep my head down. My knees hurt from kicking. My feet ache in my boots.

From atop a wobbly plastic stool at Wal-Mart, I've chosen my boots from the last shelf, high over my head. From my perch I survey all the place owns – the CD aisle, women's wear, fabrics and notions, the electronics all locked up, housewares housewares housewares, artificial Christmas trees already and decorations galore, even the carrot tops of the cashiers from the neighbouring working-class towns of Westville and Stellarton. These women are glad to have jobs here, at Wal-Mart where there are greeters and price slashings and the promise of tomorrow. Some of them lost brothers, husbands, and sons in the Westray mine disaster a decade before; one of the younger women who works here lost her father and still dreams of him most nights.

The Westray story is still told here. It always will be told, because it's unforgettable; how before dawn one May morning in 1992, a blast rocked the tiny community of Plymouth, just east of Stellarton, shattering windows all the way to New Glasgow. It came from the depths of the coal mine, fierce and hard and merciless, blowing away the top of the mine entrance more than a mile above, demolishing the steel roof supports throughout the tunnels underground. The bodies of eleven of the twenty-six miners it killed still lie in the tunnels today. The oldest was fifty-six; the youngest twenty-two, and the region had seen their like before. Nearly three hundred Pictou County miners have died over the years in methane-and-coal-dust explosions like the one that brought down Westray, and many of those worked the same rich Foord seam that became part of Westray's doom. Over the years another three hundred men, and more, have been dispatched by other methods: chewed up in machinery, buried under stone, mashed between coal cars.

The Westray miners had names like Benoit, Drolet, Feltmate, Gillis, MacKay, MacNeil, the names of the people we pass today in the supermarket or read about on the church and society pages of the local newspaper. One was called Romeo. Wherefore art thou now, Romeo, above ground or below? They pulled down just over $800 a week, a startling wage for these parts. Many pulled down more. The money at Westray was good if you worked overtime; if you worked fast, and blindly, and without an eye for the future.

My father was supposed to be on that night shift along with the twenty-six others. He was on his way back from holidays with my mother. They had gone to Boston, and my dad felt they spent too much money. They both decided that he would work overtime when they got back to New Glasgow. Not sure what prevented them from arriving on time for shift change, but he arrived back somewhere around seven or eight pm. . . . just missing the six pm change.

For the owners, the money was better. The Foord seam reserves were unusually thick, with low sulphur content and a high BTU rating, and were estimated at forty-five million tons. But the seam was geographically faulted so that mine roofs collapsed. It was choked with methane too, and had problems of spontaneous combustion quite apart from those caused by sparking machinery. Who cared? Five days before a provincial election in Nova Scotia, Curragh Resources of Toronto announced the creation of the mine and three hundred new jobs. The next day the province ponied up with a $12-million loan. A week later, Nova Scotia Power announced it would buy 700,000 tons of coal a year for fifteen years at a guaranteed price. The Bank of Nova Scotia kicked in a $100-million loan, of which the federal government guaranteed the lion's share.

Pictou County is a place of cavalier disregard, of operators and political opportunism, of oblivion. It's where we live now, stymied at every turn; it's where we can't find a map; it's where we can't get along. We have walked to and fro through the earth, as Zecariah said, and behold, all of Pictou County sitteth still. The drivers on the streets are slow, spaced out at the traffic lights; the shoppers in the towns stand and stare and block the aisles of the stores with their carts as if they're the only ones in the place. It's as if North America's first batch of chloroform, produced here a century and a half ago, has hung on in a cloud. This is a population that puts up with things, expects to have to. Brian Mulroney needed a safe Conservative seat from which to be launched into the House of Commons, and was elected from here before he became Prime Minster of Canada. Down he came from Quebec, with Mila, to do the barbecue circuit with the incumbent who had stepped aside, and he disappeared thereafter, sending back a gift – the Westray mine. The provincial premier on the Westray watch, also a Conservative, had also been elected from Pictou; he went on afterwards to a $120,000 salary as the Canadian Consul to Boston. Pictou County still votes Conservative, as if none of it mattered, how in the few months of the Westray mine's life government inspectors looked the other way at the miners' poor training; how the crazy arrangement of tunnels forced them into risky places to get the coal out faster; how the shoddy ventilation couldn't contain the gas and the flammable dust; how methane detectors were disconnected because they were always going off; and how safety drills lapsed until inspections threatened.

Worked underground with Larry knew him well. Glad there was memorial people should have been held accountable Big cover up again

The families of the dead sued the province, but the Nova Scotia Supreme Court ruled it protected under the Workers Compensation Act. Curragh was charged, and declared bankruptcy. The charges were off, then on, then off again. The Crown went after the mine managers for criminal negligence and manslaughter, only to fold during its prosecution. Company officials boycotted the public inquiry, which had no federal powers and could not enforce subpoenas in Toronto. And the miners who died? In some corners, they were blamed for working so much overtime that it made them slack, maybe even a little stupid.

•_

All these years later, a radio station is playing directly from the PA over my head, at eye level with the Wal-Mart rubber boot shelf. It's a Top-40 station at the top of the hour, and the news is on now. The local news, the national news, sometimes even world news if a plane's gone down or a whale's been rescued, and especially the financial news – it seems all the more significant for its proximity; it's like a voice from God. *There's pent-up demand*, God says as I hunt down my size of rubber boot. *Weakening asset values in financial markets could signal or precipitate an excessive softening in household and business spending.*

In boots spending, how about that?

But it's less I want since I've been in Diamond, not more. I need a size, and once I find it, I'm going home. It's just gumboots I want, nothing more. I'm having to slop through mud. I'm having to march the fields, dodging bullets, hoping for a sign; and yes, I'm having someone die. It's less of this I want, and more of life, and, as if she knows that, a Wal-Mart clerk appears, scolding me. She's not a greeter. *Get down from there!* she says. *Get down from there! You could get us all sued.*

·✦

It's weeks before I stop searching the fields for him, covertly, out of the corner of my eye lest anyone find me sentimental. It's clear I'm not suited to country life, where the wolf or at least the coyote is quite literally at your door, stalking your feathery and furry things. In the Hobbesian barnyard at Diamond, *no arts; no letters; no society; and which is worst of all, continual fear and danger of violent death; and the life of duck, solitary, poor, nasty, brutish, and short.*

The Scott paper mill in the town of Pictou is said to have brought the coyotes in, to keep the local rabbits from eating the seedlings the company transplanted into the wilds. No one complains, though the sheep farmers lose livestock every season, we lose ducks, and everyone loses sleep as the coyotes pass by, yipping and caterwauling in the night. Rover and Fluffy go down too, sooner or later once they go out. But it's politically incorrect to fault the mill on any point, not for the deaths, not for the clear-cutting, not for the blot it makes on the shore of Pictou's otherwise pristine, historical, tourist-hopeful harbour, not even for the stench that some days hangs in the air as far away as Truro, an hour's drive south toward Halifax.

Who's this guy Scott who owns all the land around the farm?

We wondered that when we saw our deed for the first time. He's our friend, that's who; along with his stink, his ravaged roads, his coyotes, and the roar of his chainsaws comes work.

But who brought the foxes in, and the eagles and the raccoons? "You can thin out your visitors, you know," says Gordon McLeod, who's been farming in nearby Rockfield all his life. "Get yourself a shotgun."

Some nights when the raccoons come by, whooping it up under the bird feeders, I go down and snap the porch light on and off, rattle the door. Three, four in the morning. B has a skunk gun. I never touch it, but I have stepped outside and thrown a watering can at them. They look up from their snack and eye me blankly, limpidly; then they trade glances with each other. They're unflappable. Look, Jimmy, one seems to say to the other. Dinner *and* a show.

I hate the raccoons. I hate the coyotes, the foxes, the skunks – but I'm sad for them too. I hate seeing them flattened into the shoulders of the road. I hate the eagles too. How do *they* get to be protected? "The ducks just sit there, waiting to be preyed on," I complain to B, as if he can do anything about it. I won't let him use his gun either. "They just sit there like –"

"Sitting ducks?"

I'm far too fond of animals to own them. Every acquisition becomes a Buddhist lesson in non-attachment, and I never learn it. After Festus disappears, a friend tries to cheer me up. Viaduc? he writes. As Chico said in some Marx Brothers movie, Vy not a chicken?

Vy not a chicken? One Hughie Fortune, sideburns and a ball-cap, pulls up in a white pickup shortly after we arrive at Diamond, asking if we'd like his hens. Hughie's going on a trip; he feels it's too much to hope to find someone who'll feed them while he's away. He has a little black-and-white Bantam that lays daily.

The way he talks about her, with affection, warns me off. There'd be another lesson in non-attachment coming soon to my neighbourhood if I took her in, that was clear: she'd be my little Bantam in no time, then she'd be gone. Eagles, hawks, foxes, raccoons. Black and white. Textbook.

·⤳

Festus is gone. Just when we thought we had nine ducks, we have only eight. Now, those eight have become couch potatoes. The cold's been settling in on Diamond over the last week, and they've voted their disapproval by retiring to the barn for days on end. It's unconscionable of them, in my view, not to go out now after all the worrying I did over them those nights not so long ago when they refused to come *in*.

It's one of the last days of Indian summer, late this year at the very end of November. They should be out on a day like this, we agree; they need some fresh air. We sound like my mother. I block the doorway to their sleeping quarters, a small partitioned corner of the barn, while B chases the raucous little band round all three walls of the great room and finally out the door. They're dismayed. They regroup on the far side of the barn, discussing their options. They send a scout around to the front. She reports back; door's shut. Defeated, they file down the bank to the little creek that winds along beside the barn on its way past the house.

And then, for a duck heading into winter, everything's new again. Nothing is as fine as unexpected water, nothing as sublime. It beads through the air and catches the light. They run up to the overhanging rocks and jump in; they climb out and run up to the rocks again. They dive, they crow, they stand up in the stream and clap their wings, they splash each other. Sometimes they fight. One more step up the evolutionary ladder and no doubt they'll be holding each others' heads under, they'll be turning a blind eye, suing, finger-pointing, *you worked overtime! you turned off the alarms! you signed the loans!*, there'll be the big cover-up again, but for now they pummel and churn the stream through their wing tips, *wak-wak*.

I stand for a long time on the old plank bridge over the creek, at a discreet distance where they won't feel they're being watched. Tricked by the heat of the day, iridescent young spiders wake in the long, decaying grass around the bridge, yawn, launch themselves on silk threads from the tips of the bleached stalks. They hang in the air, ballooning; they're gone.

I sit down on the bridge, quietly, dangling my feet over the side. I count the ducks. Eight. Only eight.

Eight still.

There's a big, fat full moon outside that night, slung low on the horizon and the colour of curry. We go out with the binoculars to have a look. It must mean something, and I wish on it.

Lying in bed, we imagine him somewhere over Jacksonville. "He's sipping a mint julep on a beach," B says. "At his side an American Black Duck, a real black beauty."

We imagine him returning next spring, sporting a tan.

•⌣

"This is not my idea of palliative care," Carol says.

She seldom starts a conversation any more, only responds when she has to, and I'm startled by the sound of her voice. I turn away from the window where I've been standing, watching the church and the Bowl-A-Rama and the parking lot between them. They all sit in a row below the window, on Pleasant Street. The hospital itself is the last building in the row. Pleasant Street, I've been thinking, isn't my idea of palliative care either. It belongs on a Monopoly board, not here. The Bowl-A-Rama too.

I walk over to her bed, take her hand. It's dry and hot, as it always is these days. Touching her is like touching the desert. A woman is burning up for want of some balm – just a little water, perhaps – that any of us should be able to give, and can't. Only her scalp is damp. Her hair is black weeds stuck down on her forehead and temples. There are still days when I think about washing it – I don't know how I'd manage it, I know it's irrational – and running a curling iron through it. Her ring will have to come off her finger soon, and come to me, before she can't remove it for swelling.

Now that you're gone
All that's left is a band of gold
All that's left of the dream I hold
Is a band of gold
And the memories of what love could be
If you were still here with me

"Nope, not my idea."
"What is, then?"
For days now she's been saving energy by talking in single words, staccato phrases. "Loved ones. Gathered. Window open just a bit, it's fall. I know that. Curtain lifting. Breeze. Lace curtain. Drifting." She lifts her hand, limply, and pushes it away from her against the air, as if something's closing in on her. "I want to drift."

I want to drift. It's a complete sentence, her constant refrain, and the doctors and nurses ignore it. We've made the mistake of asking for Demerol. Carol had it initially, the night she was admitted through Emergency after collapsing over the last Thanksgiving dinner she was to make for her family. It's been the best thing of all for her pain, she said, and wasn't too hard on her mind either. Looking back I can see myself still, bouncing out the door of her room with this news in hand, like Tigger in search of Extract of Malt. I'm running down the hall to the nursing station, buttonholing her nurse. "Carol would like some Demerol, please." Demerol, morphine, Dilaudid – what was the difference? She liked Demerol the best, so Demerol was what we wanted.

There's a big difference, as it turns out, just because of the reputation the drug has in hospitals. The hearts of the nursing staff harden at our request. It's not till weeks later, when I come across an old episode of ER on TV, that I understand why. An elderly woman had come to Cook County Emergency with a splitting headache.

"I'll get the doctor to order you a shot of sumatriptan," says Nurse Carol Hathaway. She's ever in love with on-again off-again George Clooney, Dr. Doug Ross, but Nurse Hathaway is never less than clear-eyed about her ward duties.

"Oh no, I can't take that suma stuff," says the patient. "It gives me chest pain."

"Well then, I'll get you some Cafergot."

"Cafergot makes me barf something awful. But once I had something for my migraine . . . worked like a charm . . . what was it called? Started with a D, I think . . ."

Nurse Hathaway stops dead, rolls her eyes, storms off to the nursing desk, leafs through her fat card file of ER repeats, hangers-on, and drug abusers. She pulls a card. Wait till she tells Doug about this! The old girl's been in several times lately under a variety of assumed injuries, aches, and pains. She's been given Demerol and sent home. Nurse Hathaway can't believe she almost missed her. She worries she's losing her nose for frauds and users.

Demerol's earned its reputation as a highly abused drug simply because it's often more available to addicts than are heroin and morphine, the opioids of choice. You can almost always get Demerol from your family doctor, at least once. It becomes a handy substitute for stuff you can't get. It may not be as strong a painkiller as morphine, with an analgesic potency, by comparison, of only about 10 per cent. But it has a more rapid onset and a shorter duration. It's also more sedating than an equally analgesic dose of morphine.

Maybe Carol finds that getting a shot of Demerol is like getting a quick hit of help, however brief. Is that so bad?

Apparently, it is.

"She'd like to drift," I tell anyone who'll listen. "She's very depressed. She's very anguished. She'd like something to ease her mind. Can't she have something for that?" Coming from Vancouver, it doesn't seem like such a tall order. Just about the entire population of the downtown eastside is on something like it. *Drift drugs.* It becomes our theme. Why shouldn't it? Isn't it the hospital's theme too, some sort of stated objective? It is; we read about it in the palliative unit's brochure. That's what they're prescribing here, though clearly it doesn't include pain relief: *comfort and dignity for the ill person as well as the best quality of life for the patient and the patient's caregivers.*

There's always a sentinel duck standing guard while the others feed. He stands tall on his orange legs, his head swivelling to imagined dangers. He's my counterpart in the duck world, vigilant and ineffectual. He can't stop it when it comes, and even with a heads up and a head start they're not fast enough to get away anyway. But he'll have seen it coming. He'll have told them so. It's his only virtue.

⌣

Comfort. Dignity. Drift drugs. But we didn't want that at all, as it turned out – not, at least, the hospital's version. Though I didn't know it then, what we wanted was what science calls an ataractic, a drug or a drug mix that induces serenity. Work on ataractics began back in the 1940s, when pharmacologists and anaesthesiologists found they could use antihistamines to make barbiturates even more sedating. In the 1950s, they discovered that chlorpromazine (the choice antipsychotic agent Thorazine) could do the same thing. This is a drug with little analgesic effect itself that nonetheless brings it out in others. It's said, therefore, to have an *adjuvant* effect, and adding Thorazine to morphine or Demerol means you can get away with less morphine or Demerol and still control pain. With an adjuvant, morphine or Demerol can control pain at a dose that doesn't also risk respiratory depression.

But the combination left patients sluggish and toxic, as did the combination of morphine and promethazine (Phenergan), an antihistamine that has the added value of causing moderate sedation and centrally mediated antiemesis. (That is, it stops nausea and vomiting, by working directly on the brain.) Still, the three drugs – Demerol + Phenergan + Thorazine, or "DPT" – became a popular cocktail for sedating and anaesthetizing surgical patients. It remains popular today.

At the same time, other, better ataractic approaches were coming into their own. *Neuroleptanalgesia* is what medical science calls the indifference to pain that comes from taking a potent analgesic along with a neurolept, or major tranquilizing drug. ("I still feel it," I say to B when I've finally drugged down a migraine. "It's just that I don't care about it any more.") The Frenchmen whose work led eventually to neuroleptanalgesia complained that DPT brought on a kind of artificial hibernation, associated with overlong bouts of unconsciousness and cardiovascular instability.

The 1940s, the 1950s: it's the millennium already, so let's get on with it. Whatever the mix and whatever the side effects, it seems there are plenty of drift drugs out there.

None of this did I know then. And it wouldn't have mattered if I had. *Drift drugs, my friend would like drift drugs*, I say; I'm a broken record.

The nurses are stony-faced. They're a brick wall. "We don't get into that until the end," they say. "She's getting clonazepam for euphoria anyway."

For *euphoria*?

"Pffft," Carol says.

I hunt through her drug orders to find the one for euphoria. Clonazepam is a relatively new benzodiazapene, one of the many minor tranquilizers related to valium. Officially it's billed as an antiseizure drug, but it's good for relaxation, sleep. It has drift possibilities, I suppose, and I decide to test it for myself. I take one of Carol's at bedtime.

I haven't had much balance for years – not since my several bouts of labyrinthitis, a viral infection of the inner ear that has made me chronically dizzy, and whose effects in me have lingered as lifelong clumsiness and blundering, especially in the dark. In the country, that's been a handicap. There's no night light anywhere, and B has to take me down every dark path we go. I've been stiffening up with middle age for years too; every bone in my body hurts, and my joints are going. But I was not always as you see me now; I was limber once. It's been at least thirty years since I took ballet lessons with my sister, when we were little girls. At least thirty years since the *pliés* in first, second, fourth, and fifth at the *barre*, the *battements tendu*, the foot pushes, *dégagés, pas de chevals*, the *rond de jambe á terre*, the *battements frappé et fondu*, even the wobbly *arabesques* – and then, *Class! Let's put it all together!* the Waltz of the Fairies, the Spanish Dance, Prairie Dance, Ragdoll Dance, Chinese Dance, Farmer's Polka, and Merry Marching Majorettes. I endured most of those, but I loved the time we were angels, with wings, in the Christmas concert. Margie Flemming scuffed her slipper on a patch of floor that never should have been polished in the first place and fell off the stage into the audience with a shriek, but I was an angel and I had wings and I picked up my feet and kept right on going. The place was in an uproar around Margie, and I kept on going. *This is as close as I'm getting to glory, I'm keeping on regardless* – already, I had a sense of that.

But now, aren't I close now? I feel I am. Drifting on this small, round bit of orange from one of Carol's many pill bottles, I find that as the lights go down I've wandered onto some stage, resplendent in pink shoes, pink tights, pink tutu. There's applause distantly, or a wave of something else like heat or pleasure. My feet are the size of a six-year-old's. They're fluid and oiled and they move in small, graceful sweeps. There's no pain in them anywhere. In the distance, over the applause, the opening strains of the second act of *Swan Lake*, the haunting of the oboe. There must be an orchestra pit somewhere. Above it, on the apron of the stage, I'm *first position to second, point. Second position to third, point.* The *recitatif* of the ballet mistress lulls me. My arms follow my feet, and my head inclines with my arms, following each in turn. I'm Giselle, I'm Odile the black swan, I'm up in a pirouette, then down in an arabesque. I'm extended, graceful, stretching myself into a splendid line I know by heart, can find again and again without looking, at a moment's notice, with a turn of a chin, at the cadence of a note. I move perfectly, as I was taught thirty years before and as I've not recalled a single time since, till now. It's as if the body has a memory all its own.

But the stage disappears, then, and the stage lights too, and I've wandered into a vast green meadow, warm between cool mountains. I'm running in the meadow, I'm spinning so hard that the mountain air rushes in my ears. My arms are wide and I'm laughing as if I've jumped from the lap of God to play a bit before I climb back on. I'm singing now, I'm whirling and the mountains are tumbling round me and I'm not dizzy in the least; a black-and-white-striped pinafore bib seems to grow up my chest toward my throat, and before I turn utterly into Julie Andrews in *The Sound of Music* I fall asleep.

None of this happens to Carol when she takes clonazepam – not even sleep, except when she takes large doses. She takes three at bedtime, and during the day a half or a whole one p.r.n. – as necessary, or on demand. And still it only makes her feel dopier, more sluggish, more depressed, because as the last of her capabilities leaves her she is more and more inconsolable. She sees how much she's lost. On the clonazepam, she feels more a dead weight than ever.

Clonazepam. Supplied: 0.5 mg. Each cylindrical, biplane, scored tablet, edges bevelled, contains: clonazepam 0.5 mg. (orange, with RIVOTRIL *0.5 engraved on one face, single-scored on the other with* ROCHE *above and C below score). Also contains lactose, micro-crystalline cellulose, cornstarch, sunset yellow* FCF *aluminum lake, magnesium stearate.*

Aluminum lake is a dye, from the French *laque* (where we get lacquer), created by an interaction with aluminum ions. It's used in food, cosmetics, pharmaceuticals. Even though it brings her no peace and she finds it a bitter pill to swallow, some days we still manage to get through to evening and sleep, sitting together and drifting on that sunset yellow lake.

•‿

It was the way I felt with Zelda when times were good, in that warm lap of meadow between those cool mountains, and when it died I would not have thought such a long-time friend could lay me down so low, so fast, could drop me there and walk away without a word. I would've thought there'd still be some brief thing worth saying, a joke to share between us, a small, nervous laugh – that one day she'd reach up again and brush the hair out of my eyes; *Dawnio*, she'd say. *Let's forget the whole thing.* It was her tenderness that I loved, her guilelessness. She seemed the sort of innocent who couldn't lie even to save someone's feelings. She wouldn't know blarney if she fell over it into a deep hole.

I mistook these things for purity, when all the time it was hardness, and it was there to see.

I should have seen it in the relationships she left in her wake – the three ex-husbands, the discarded boyfriends, the kids who couldn't wait to grow up and get away to school, all of these calling her *madwoman! bitch!* more often than you hear these days in family life. The lack of friends, and then the friendships that survived only because she felt she should be courteous or could not give offence. Claudia, deranged, attacking the kitchen table over and over, the table strewn over the kitchen floor so that the whole summer long there was never a place to eat. The estranged father, the brothers Zelda hadn't spoken to in years except for the one in England whom she never saw and consequently still liked. Even her mother, dead twenty-five years of cancer, who came to her regularly in dreams, not to reminisce but to strangle her.

Could the faults have lain with everyone but herself? If I'd only looked sooner. There it was, staring me in the face.

> *A sad misfortune came o'er me*
> *Which caused me to stray from the land*
> *Far away from my friends and relations*
> *Betrayed by the black velvet band*
>
> *Her eyes they shone like diamonds*
> *I thought her the queen of the land*
> *And her hair hung over her shoulder*
> *Tied up with a black velvet band*

Diamonds are used to test the hardness of other materials. One special kind of tester, the Shore scleroscope, measures the strength or hardness of a substance's elasticity. A diamond-tipped hammer in a graduated glass tube falls on the test specimen, whose hardness is told by the height to which the hammer rebounds. The harder the material, the higher the rebound.

The Shore is a fancy machine. The well-known Mohs hardness measure, however, named after a scale devised in 1812 by the German mineralogist Friedrich Mohs, is merely a scratch test. If something is scratched by the mineral calcite (number three on the Mohs scale) but not by gypsum (number two), its Mohs hardness is two-and-a-half to three. With a Mohs hardness of two plus, your fingernails won't quite be scratched by gypsum. Glass is about five-and-a-half, diamonds are ten.

Zelda is harder.

⤳

My friend Joel's little boy Jonah is one, and he's afraid of ducks. No one knows where this came from, just as my mother has no idea how I got my spider phobia. It's here, though, that's the thing; it will have to be borne. Joel will have to start using my mother's lines on his son. She'd say *don't be silly, Jonah, those ducks are far more frightened of you than you are of them.*

It's the line she used to use on me for spiders. See how well it worked.

When they're not out sailing, the ducks live in our smaller, newer barn, the one closer to the house. The old barn is a bit of a distance for a duck. It lies on the far side of the brook that only veers close when it gets near the house, where it winds down under our kitchen window. Many, many years ago, if its state of disrepair today is an indication, some homesteader laid a plank bridge over the brook at the point where it wanders away from the house, toward the old barn. The bridge is ancient, but plenty wide for a truck or a hay wagon to pass over, going back and forth between the barns. The ducks don't cross it, but when the weather cools, while it's still warm enough for the brook to flow, they abandon the pond in the south field, by the road, and hold court under its planks.

I love this bridge, as I do any bridge. A bridge is to build, to dream on, to dive from, to look off of, forward and backward, to sit on, to dangle from, to guard. A bridge is a suspension. I love these few rickety planks of ours, and I love those six-lane feats of engineering you find in cities. A bridge is to cross, after all, and yet it's never straightforward, never without its little joke. In cities, bridges bottleneck, and they cost. They're never without their traffic or their tolls. A bridge eliminates the obstacle of the stream, the lake, the chasm, the death drop – and it adds in another. There isn't a bridge in a children's fairytale that doesn't have an impossible tariff thrown in for good measure – a hideous, hungry troll, more often than not, just to make life difficult.

As kids we have to learn it fast, that you can't get there from here, not without tremendous trouble, not even from one end of the stage to the other. Just look at Margie Flemming at the Christmas concert. You might even have to give up your very own best buddies to get across. Maybe a sacrifice will be demanded of you, sometimes a betrayal. There's danger everywhere, not to mention retribution, and sometimes the troll makes you give up your best friend. *I'm so small and bony and I don't taste very good either . . . why don't you wait for the next of us three little billy-goats, who is much fatter and juicier than me?*

It's a dreadful thought I get stuck on when I'm a kid, this idea of unnatural selection, of arbitrary culling. This idea of death at all. I think of what I'd give up to save myself. My sister? Many a time she and I did the kid's meditation, riding in the back of the car after we've overdosed on counting licence plates.

How would you rather die? Burning to death or freezing to death?

Freezing.

Being hanged or being guillotined?

Hanged. And it's GEE-*oh-teened, not* GILL-*oh-teened.*

Whatever. Drawn or quartered?

They're the same thing.

They are not.

Are so, dummy. You do them together.

You do not.

Girls. Our mother, from the front seat.

However you cut it, it's an awful thought. *The rafters are falling, Mom,* I'd press her. *Fire's raining down on our heads. You can only grab one of us. Who do you pick?*

How does anyone cross to safety?

At Diamond we have ducks under our bridge, not trolls. It's where they take their meetings, all talking at once, it's where they think they can't be seen, and they abandon it faster than a house on fire when they hear one of us coming.

Ducks never feel safe, it seems, and ours give every indication they think we're axe murderers even though they hardly give us a chance, even though all they really know about us is that we feed them and change their linen. Perhaps their skepticism is no surprise. The ducks you buy at the store, from the freezer case, have been raised in pens by the tens of thousands, and live exactly forty-nine days. *Nasty, brutish, and short.*

"They're not exactly friendly," says B. "Nothing worse than an uppity duck." He shovels the duck pen – I don't, there being a tapestry of webs in the barn – and once when he broke the ice on the stream for them in his unemployment boots, he fell in. As the weeks go by and the temperatures drop, the straw-and-guano mix that coats the duck-barn floor freezes into concrete, and B makes unsavoury remarks about ducksicles and ducks-on-sticks.

Now that Festus is gone, it seems the ducks are B's nemesis, as is nearly everything on Diamond Farm.

⸱⤙

According to a survey in *Time* magazine, only 1 per cent of us think that good sex is the key to a strong marriage. Most of us think, instead, that communication is what counts. My B is a man of few words. The only time I've seen him chatty it's been kidney stone season again, and he's been drugged to neuroleptanalgesia in the ER of the Royal Columbia Hospital in Vancouver. Once he caught himself on fire, cooking breakfast on a gas stove in his terry robe, and the first I knew about it was the sound of a plate he'd dropped on the floor as it shattered.

"Survey says the second most important thing in a happy marriage is wiring," he tells me. "That and plumbing." Eben, the electrician who works steady at the Michelin Tire plant in town but who moonlighted for us on a couple jobs when we arrived, fails to return to wire the bathroom. Other tradesmen in the vicinity are booking months down the road, as if they're rheumatologists or cardiologists. My mother, ever the proponent of self-actualization, plies B with Black & Decker and Time-Life books: *Ask the Family Handyman, Exterior Home Repairs & Improvements, House Framing, Basic Wiring.* Even *Ultimate Decks* and *Wind Energy Basics* for his leisure moments.

"I'd like to live somewhere else," B growls, on one of his Sparky days. It takes four of these to finish the bathroom. I've been thinking I should get him a tool belt – the big, saggy kind the apartment super Schneider used to wear on that old Valerie Bertinelli sitcom, *One Day at a Time.*

"Want to go back to Vancouver?"

"Hardly," he snorts. "At least we've got a house here. Or we will, eventually. In Vancouver, there were about two buildings in the whole place that didn't look like they'd been assembled overnight with a glue gun in a parking lot."

"Where, then?" *I'd live in Nuttby, that's what I think.* We pass the sign for the Old Nuttby Road when we take the back roads to the city to see Carol. New Nuttby is four houses strung alongside the battered asphalt, a boarded-up fire hall, and, at night, on our way home, two or three oncoming cars that invariably fail to dim their lights as they pass. But the residents of Nuttby can be forgiven most anything, I imagine. I love the name. Nuttby even has a sign to mark it, more than Diamond does. I long to enlist.

Not B. "Thief River Falls, Minnesota," he says. That's where he'd rather be.

"What's in Thief River Falls, Minnesota?"

"Nothing that's in Diamond, that's what."

What else don't we know? Charlie, who's worked on the house, feeds us bad news slowly, an item at a time, as if we've been down with flu, awake ravenous, and need restraining from the table. Scarlet and Jo had no water in the winter, except when they raised the trapdoor, took the two hairdryers and the extension cords they kept bundled on the top step of the stairs down to the root cellar, and thawed the water lines. We're in a wind tunnel, a frost zone, a snow belt, a flood belt. A river runs under the house that will need a dam to keep it away. And because of it, the cellar already needs a couple thousand dollars' work before freeze-up.

B is worn down by Diamond by the time the cat enters our lives, and I'm worn down by heartache. Otherwise, things might have gone better.

⁓

The emergency room of the Aberdeen Hospital in New Glasgow is much like any other ER on a Sunday night – packed. Its redemption lies in a large colour TV mounted high on the wall, for the benefit of those patients who won't be seen for several hours, as well as for the staff who'd otherwise be complained to. B watches Superchannel, Arnold Schwarzenegger and James Belushi duking it out with the New York City underworld. We're mired for hours among squalling infants, stoical, withered old men in workboots, buckling jeans, and ball caps, and pickled teenagers who've banged themselves up in every way possible. There's coughing everywhere; the room is racked with fits of it.

I keep my head down, trying to finish the murder mystery I've pocketed on the way out the door. Nothing like a medical emergency to help you catch up on your reading. God knows when I'll get such quiet time again. My book is a fat paperback, and it needs two hands to hold it open. Sadly, I have only one functioning. After only a couple hours, the other is already swollen to twice its size. I've been bitten by a cat.

Charles Dickens' *Great Expectations* is the story of the young hero Pip and his secret benefactor – a convict (it turns out later) named Magwitch. When Magwitch escapes from prison and flees into the night, hungry, he trips over Pip, playing on the moor. The boy brings the frightful wretch some food, without any idea who he is. It's a good turn that will reward him. A terrifying, simple man, Magwitch may have a long memory for his enemies, but he remembers his friends too. After that first night on the moor, he goes on to make good his escape – and to make it very good: he prospers, and from a distance and anonymously, he opens doors for Pip, by then a young man. All good things must come to an end, though, and eventually old enemies inform on him. With Magwitch's secret out, Pip's great expectations fade, and misfortune comes upon him. Guilty by association, he falls penniless. *Great Expectations* is not always a happy story.

None of which matters to our Magwitch, the ratty grey stray who's adopted us – except for the first part: the part about the moors, the desolation, the hunger, the rescue. Perhaps Diamond was always her home. She bunked at least a season in the duck barn before we even discovered her, living off duck eggs. No wonder the ducks blame us for everything.

Then one day she walked out into the yard and sat there in the pouring rain, looking up at the windows and crying. Dirt ran off her in muddy rivulets, blending into the puddles.

A fearful man, all in coarse grey, with a great iron on his leg. A man with no hat, and with broken shoes, and with an old rag tied round his head. A man who had been soaked in water, and smothered in mud, and lamed by stones, and cut by flints, and stung by nettles, and torn by briars; who limped, and shivered, and glared, and growled; and whose teeth chattered in his head as he seized me by the chin.

We already have a Smike, after the sweet but hapless creature in *Nicholas Nickelby* who suffers the watering down of the milk, the attenuation of the gruel, and general squalor all round at Mr. Squeers' Home for Boys, which B says is like Diamond Farm any day of the week – *Dotheboys Hall, at the delightful village of Dotheboys. . . . No extras, no vacations, and diet unparalleled.* As I explain to people who see the cat now, ample, glossy, very spoiled, and preening in the sun after lunch, we saw him first as a derelict kitten at the shelter, and he seemed Smike-like at the time.

Smike's taken, so Magwitch it is for the stray, but not for long. It turns out that Magwitch is a girl and needs a name change.

It's just as well. B can't get his tongue around Magwitch. *Mugwitch, Mugwall, Mugwash, Muggy:* she gets called everything. One day I hear this: *Murgatroyd, can you spell taxidermist?* They haven't been getting along, what with the cat yowling at all hours and making a run on the door every time it opens, to get inside.

Magwitch has her Ancient Mariner story too: *I was not always as you see me now.* She's been someone's pet not long before, that's certain by her mournful sweetness, and she intends to be one again. One fine fall evening when we have the windows open, she flings herself seven feet straight up from the grass and hangs from the trim outside the dining room. She's like the ghost of Catherine Earnshaw trying to claw her way back into her Wuthering Heights home. The sounds coming out of her are sepulchral. Inside the house, Smike and Frankie launch themselves in counterattack against the window screen, and everything on the sill comes crashing down. Carol's tiny chintz-painted pots, the ones she brought as a housewarming gift on the only visit she'll ever make to Diamond, are demolished in the dust-up, and I spend the evening piecing them back together with glue and a toothpick.

B is especially upset by the loss of the pots, even though he's immune to the feel of prescience or a haunting. Me, on the other hand: I'm a woman, I'm an adult, things get broken, people die, *been there done that get over it get over it.*

I say it to myself all night. Tears drip off my nose.

B starts the clock running on Mugwall, Mugwash, Muggy. I have to get her out of here before she turns into a Patsy or a Twinkie or a Fluff. Or just a fond, howling memory, a greasy spot. We put notices in the neighbours' mailboxes: *Great mouser free to good home.* I design them with scrolled borders and curlicues and wingdings and print them off on pink paper; B drives them up and down the road. Lots of government cheques in those mailboxes, he reports. No response to our notices. At least a dozen strays get dumped off every year, on this and all the other back roads in the county; what's one more? We've got to be kidding. B himself has seen it first-hand, rounding the first turn of the Diamond Road one day where vehicles can no longer be seen from the 256. He nearly ran him down, the man in the shirtsleeves and tie from town who'd just disembarked his SUV, dog in his arms, to pitch the little terrier into the woods and speed away.

We must proceed, I say, *as if we can make a difference, even if we think we can't.* We visit my family for Sunday dinner. "Listen," I say, "we have to package the cat. We have to find her a home. Names, anyone?"

"*Brit*ney, Na*tash*a," the boys sing-song.

"Screech," says B.

"Thank you all," I say coldly. "Thank you all ever so very much."

"Molly," says my mother, and passes the beets.

But no one wants Molly, however finely packaged. Even the New Glasgow SPCA won't take adult cats, not that I'd put her there. I would hurl myself between this cat and death and I don't know why until someone tells me: *You can't save Carol, but you can save Mol.*

We spar over her. Suddenly, every difference of opinion is over a cat.

"Why the hell do we have to hustle her out? She ate the damn squirrel, after all."

"She did not. The squirrel left."

"Like hell he left. Wild horses weren't going to drag him out. He'd moved in, lock, stock, and barrel. He'd sent for Mrs. Squirrel and the kids. He was holed up for the winter, and his hide-a-bed and his washer-spindryer too." It was true. He'd been a noisy squirrel while he lasted, waking us mornings before dawn as if he were a fully fleshed human roomer in the flat above, just trying to get in a little tidying up before work.

The squirrel has been another sore spot. We couldn't let him nest in the roof over the winter, and we especially couldn't let him start a family there. They'd ruin our R-2000 and eat the insulation on the wiring. For some reason, squirrels love wiring. B wanted to shoot him. I insisted we try a humane trap from the Havahart Small Animal Trap Co. We got a junior cage with a one-way door loaded on springs. We baited it with apples and peanut butter. The squirrel ignored it.

Soon after we make a bed for Molly in the mudroom out of a packing carton I cut down and line with one of the heavy packing blankets the movers left behind, the squirrel disappears.

Molly lives in the mudroom and cries at the door. The temperature drops with every passing day, and when I pick her up in the morning I can smell the frost on her.

Maybe we can take her in ourselves. I poke around the edges

of it with B, who's silent, sullen. In late November we set out on a walk to the old Diamond Cemetery and Molly follows, trotting along like a faithful dog. She sits on the gravestones and washes her ears, then leads the way home, tail in the air like a flagpole. It's an hour's walk there and back, and she looks like she's just getting started.

"She loves being with us," I say to B. "She loves us."

He says nothing, and he does not say no.

·⤳

Sixteen countries, all the nation-states of the South Pacific, make up the Forum of Nations. Together they govern a large chunk of the richest tuna fishing grounds in the world. To protect and manage their territory some years ago, the founding states established the Forum Fisheries Agency. They hired B for advice. For several months he travelled around the South Pacific, explaining communications, surveillance, even weapons systems. Especially weapons systems. The questions they had! A nice .50-calibre machine gun for that patrol boat? he'd say. You get those from Saco Defense up in Maine. But the Forum wanted 20mm guns, the kind you use to turn forests into parking lots and the other guys' trawlers into toothpicks. You get those from Litton Systems or General Electric, B said. Long Range Radar? Raytheon. Really fast patrol boats? Noel Riley at Commercial Marine Design in Sydney, Australia, will design those for you. He also organized system demos, and set up an encrypted radio link between the FFA headquarters in Honiara in the Solomon Islands and the Capricorn Hotel in Suva, Fiji. He strung a little wire between the balconies of adjoining rooms at the Capricorn; it served as the antenna for

the 1500-mile path. The Fijian chambermaids looked on, chattering among themselves. One evening B came in to find the radio link
snarled, the data scrambled. The maids had hung his bedsheets on
the wire to air. He had to fix it all, but it wasn't any worse than
the experience of getting into the shower the next morning and
stepping on a lizard. Under the worst circumstances, B solves problems: that's what he does.

What can we do with Molly? What can we do? I ask him
through the whole ordeal. He has no idea.

⠂⟋

Here's what's involved: getting her tested for infections and, if she
passes, getting her immunized; meanwhile, seeing what our cats
were immunized against years ago, and what still sticks. Since
they've always been indoor cats, I haven't updated their shots.
Then, getting her spayed.

Getting her to like Frankie and Smike and vice versa.

She checks out at the vet. She doesn't have any lethal infections,
and she's already been spayed. The vet looks at her teeth. She's
about a year old, and in great shape. *She was someone's pet long
ago, and she'll soon be one again.* She gets a shot. It'll need to be
updated, and we make an appointment to come back in a month.

And then the cats' face-to-face meeting at the door. It goes
rather less well than their meeting through the window screen
earlier in the fall, on that warm Indian summer night, and we never
keep that appointment at the vet.

⠂⟋

If you're bitten by a cat, you'll probably need antibiotics. The nature of the wound itself demands it – a deep puncture wound, driven hard into the recesses of your flesh by very long, very thin teeth. It will be inoculated with germs not near the skin but right at its deep end. Left untreated, it can heal over and leave you with a sunken, festering pocket of infection. You'll most likely have been bitten on the hand. Hands have too poor a blood supply to carry in good volumes of immune and antibacterial agents.

Though it might need cosmetic suturing, a slash wound is not nearly so serious – nor so common. A dog bite is usually a slash wound, and it's not usually as troublesome as a cat bite. A cat bite, though, is a walk in the park compared to a human bite. Dog bites carry about sixty-four pathogens, enough to discredit the old wives' tale that if a dog licks a scratch it's going to heal faster. Cat mouths aren't as clean as dog mouths, and carry more. A human bite, however, can transmit a whopping two hundred and fifty pathogens. That's more or less how many organisms you carry in your mouth.

Human mouths are sewers, and patients with a human bite to the hand are usually admitted to hospital for IV antibiotics. Infections of the hand of any kind are bad, and can damage job and income prospects down the road. Human bites, additionally, can transmit hepatitis B and C as well as HIV, at least theoretically – so far, no cases have been documented.

Anyone who's sustained a serious bite, especially to the face or hand, should get it looked at. A bite that breaks the skin is serious. If you don't think your bite is serious but you go on to develop a fever, or tenderness, warmth, or redness, or a red streak near the wound, you've been wrong. About one in every hundred emergency room visits is for a human or an animal bite, and most often it's kids bitten by pets, dogs in particular. Only about 5 per cent of dog bites get infected, but about half of cat bites do. They're often contaminated with *Pasteurella multocida*, a bacteria not to be fooled with.

Animal bites can cause a variety of infections, including rabies and tetanus. Tetanus, a neuromuscular disease that's often fatal, is caused by the toxins *Clostridium tetani* exudes when it grows, rather than by the bacterium itself, and you risk developing it if you haven't had a tetanus booster in the last five years. With any puncture wound, you'll probably want to update your tetanus, if you're due. Tetanus spores can live for years in soil and animal wastes. The adult organism is killed easily by air and sunlight, but the spores persist. They defy most antiseptics, don't give a toss about heat or cold. They're nearly immortal, and nearly ubiquitous. *In them, an invincible summer.* They find their way onto the food you eat, the hay your ducks sleep in, the clothes you wear, the dust under your bed. Scrub all you want – tetanus spores have been found hanging in the air of hospital operating rooms.

And so they sit and wait, for the most part, but they develop easily if they find their way into a deep human wound. Unlike most viruses, which can find in nature only a very few suitable hosts, it can bunk just about anywhere – in any warm-blooded animal. In the west, having a burn or a surgical incision puts you at risk, as does shooting drugs, but even new mothers are at risk after childbirth.

A common symptom of tetanus is stiffness in the jaw – hence "lockjaw," the familiar name. The illness can be limited to muscles around the wound, where local spasms can persist for weeks. But it can also cause general muscle spasms and stiffness as well as impaired swallowing, irritability, headache, fever, sore throat, and chills. Rigid chest muscles and throat spasms can lead to suffocation. Muscle spasms can be so severe that the body bows backward, heels arching toward head. *Tetanus!* I thought when in *The Mysterious Affair at Styles* the newly-wed and very rich Mrs. Alfred Inglethorpe is found writhing in her bed in the middle of the night. *A final convulsion lifted her from the bed, until she appeared to rest upon her head and her heels, with her body arched in an extraordinary manner. In vain Mary and John tried to administer more brandy. The moments flew. Again the body arched itself in the peculiar fashion.* But strychnine poisoning can look like tetanus, and even though tetanus is five hundred times more explosive, Agatha Christie preferred strychnine.

Rabies can be carried by dogs, skunks, bats, raccoons, o'possums, and foxes. Cats not so much, but it's possible. In the American west, squirrels rarely carry rabies but do carry bubonic plague. Plague remains rare, but rabies is on the increase. A viral infection that inflames the brain and spinal cord, rabies multiplies in the central nervous system once it's travelled along nerves from the bite. Subsequently it travels down nerves to the salivary glands and the saliva, where it can be transmitted again. Infected animals can have either "furious" rabies – the Old Yeller type – or "dumb" rabies, where local or general paralysis is prominent from the outset. Most North American cases of rabies have been transmitted by wild animals. Among them, dumb rabies is more common, but rabid nocturnal animals – bats, raccoons, foxes, skunks – may appear in daytime, "furious," and show little of their usual fear of humans.

The difficulty with rabies is knowing for sure whether you've got it. The imperative of rabies is that you can't wait to find out. The incubation period lasts at least ten days, but it may be as much as a year. A short incubation is most typical in someone who's had multiple bites, or a bite to the head or trunk. Most people show symptoms in thirty to fifty days. Though a skin sample biopsied from the neck can reveal the rabies virus under microscope, by the time it does it's too late. By the time you show symptoms, it's also too late, and the diagnosis is usually only made by examination of the brains of dead or destroyed animals.

In a few people, rabies starts as a lower leg paralysis that climbs. More often it starts as a bit of the blues. Then victims get restless and feverish with general malaise, and suddenly the site of the wound tingles. Restlessness becomes wild agitation. The patient is hypersensitive to temperature changes, noise, light. There's profuse salivation, and sometimes excruciating spasms of the throat and larynx, but no local damage; it's the brain centres that control swallowing and breathing that are affected. A breath, a small breeze, a sip of water can bring on spasms, so that someone who's infected can't drink. Dying of thirst and yet revolted by water, he may be crazed by the mention of the word. Consequently, rabies has been called hydrophobia, or fear of water. One treatment for rabies thirst before IV hydration came along was to dip the victim in a pool. In a 1765 essay the English writer Oliver Goldsmith mentions "a little boy bit in the leg, and gone down to be dipped in the salt water."

Vets, lab workers, and animal handlers, spelunkers, travellers to the Third World, where rabies in dogs is rampant – all these can get vaccinations that provide some lifelong protection. Anyone else bitten by a bat, a skunk, a raccoon, or a fox will likely get shots of antirabies vaccine on the day of exposure, and then the third, seventh, fourteenth, and twenty-eighth days thereafter, but careful cleaning of wounds and flushing of punctures is probably even more important than the shots, and shots have never helped someone who has already begun to develop symptoms. This unfortunate usually has as little as three days to live; ten at most. He'll die of asphyxia, convulsions, exhaustion, or widespread paralysis.

At the Aberdeen Hospital in New Glasgow, I ask the ER doctor about rabies.

He looks blank. "Call your vet tomorrow and ask," he says.

"Call your doctor and ask," says the vet the next day.

I develop the symptoms of rabies. Yes. No. Just a little bit, or is that just a sore neck? A few more days go by. Isn't that tingling in my hand?

The best way to deal with animal bites is not to get them in the first place. Treat all unfamiliar pets with caution. Pay attention to those BEWARE OF DOG signs. Don't approach or try to touch any wild animal, especially if it looks sick. Tell your kids not to feed or play with animals they don't know; tell them to stay clear of wild animals in particular. Don't introduce Molly to Smike and Frankie.

The Shoppers Drug Mart across from the Aberdeen Hospital is still open when we finally exit the ER. While I'm getting my clarithromycin prescription filled, a transaction that will leave me $37 poorer and with the runs for a week, I try to convince the young pharmacist that she'd love to adopt a cat.

She wouldn't, and she doesn't even ask me about my hand.

On my way out, the ER doctor asked me what the cat that bit me looked like.

"What she looked like?" It seemed a strange question. What does it matter what she looked like? Shouldn't he be concerned with what *I* look like?

"Yes. What colour."

"What colour?"

"Yes."

"Grey." I ask him why he wants to know.

"Just want to make sure it was a cat, that you could see clearly it was a cat. Not a raccoon or something."

"Oh." I'm disappointed. "I thought you might have wanted to adopt her."

I call in a favour from a friend. Molly is now in her new home in the city, with Karen, Brian, and their three little girls. They love Molly to death. She has great expectations. She eats peanut butter and watches *Hockey Night in Canada* from the middle of the living-room couch, the best seat in the house.

᠂ᴗ

I tell Carol about the cat. I don't mention the dust-up at the window, the loss of the miniature chintz pots. I don't mention the little terrier discarded on the road. I tell her about our visit to the hospital.

"Mine?"

"No, the Aberdeen."

"Scotland?"

"New Glasgow."

"Scotland, that has Glasgow. Aberdeen too. Where Bill lived." She's right, she had a friend there once so she knows for sure, but she's off-topic. So often, even when she was well enough, she felt odd man out – she didn't suffer fools, she felt a step off the pace. Forever the first Mrs. Wilcox, never the second. Never the compromiser, never the red dust settling England. She'd been grace incarnate. The only problem was, no one else had been too. *Only connect.*

She's right about Scotland, about Glasgow and Aberdeen, but these days her attention can wander. It's a tremendous effort for her to pull herself back to the world of minutiae in which the rest of us locate ourselves. But she does follow my account of rabies. Three days and you're dead; ten at most. "Imagine," she says, "dying that fast."

•‿

When it comes to hunting season, your property's not really your own. The Protection of Property Act says trespass is illegal here only if someone's tramping across your lawn under your living-room windows, or through your garden, your orchard, or your vineyard, your ploughed and seeded fields, your golf course. Additionally, if you have one, your tree plantation can be yours and yours only, and your Christmas tree lot is all yours too. But the rest of your land is up for grabs, whether you paid good money for it or not.

If you want to try to keep someone out, all the same, do it with fences. Open fields are anyone's turf, but fences are a line in the sand, and they do make good neighbours. Given a fence, Everett wouldn't have had to ask, or beg and cajole; he would have known. You can try posting signs too. Signs do you no good at all on woodlands, however, because *no person may be prosecuted if that person is on forest land and is lawfully hunting or engaged in other recreational activity.* "Forest land" means *a wooded area, forest stand, tract covered by underbrush, barren ground, marsh or bog.* Whether you own it or not. We're ratepayers of everything, masters of nothing. We have no authority in our own home; we have no purchase. We have a deed that's not worth the paper it's written on. It's why there've been no bullets through our windows. It's why those hunters smile at us so broadly when we pass them on the road. That, and their six-packs.

It's why the clear-cutters smile at us too. The sentiments of the Protection of Property Act have leached into the Forests Act. Any landowner clear-cutting more than three hectares must leave a gift behind – ten living trees left standing per hectare, called wildlife clumps, legacy trees – for the birds and animals who might live there. I'm not making this up; it's what the act says. That birds and animals don't live in the forests any longer, that they've been driven out, is not the act's concern, but it is ours. Up and down the Diamond Road, a bear disembowels everyone's garbage boxes and composters regularly, with such a nose for compost collection every second week that he might have a calendar. Even in the middle of the day you see bears on the road now, and bobcats too, and Fifis everywhere are snatched from their porches by wildcats. But these forest creatures loved their natural habitat once, and might try it again, ruined or not – that's what the government seems to think. And so you see the largesse of the loggers sticking up in the wreckage of the land like blackened old bottlebrushes or spent matchsticks. You see deadwood still standing, and a few leg- islated scrawny old trees that acid rain has already finished off. These are trees that no one wanted anyway, not even the birds and the animals. On Hangman's Beach on McNabs Island in Halifax Harbour during the Napoleonic wars, the Royal Navy used to leave the corpses of executed mutineers to rot on their gibbets in plain sight of ships coming in to port. They made the kind of state- ment the legacy trees make now, a warning and a malediction. The legacy trees are a gift only because they're a warning, and those who might hear it best don't hear it at all.

The boys who work the woods have got their earmuffs on anyway, to protect against the scream of the saws and the skidders. They're smiling. They've got work, they've got licence and favour.

Everyone's on their side but us and a few other holdouts. They sit on the right hand of mammon and God; the law says they're doing just fine. As if to confirm it, the logging czar of the Diamond Road buys himself a new truck every year. It's always the same, just newer, bigger: forest green, with an orange hazard light atop the cab. For a guy like him, so unconcerned, that light seems out of place as he patrols the road, up and down, surveying all he thinks he owns. But you never know. Maybe a bear will mistake him for a composter someday and jump him, and he'll become the accident that's waiting to happen now.

᛫᎓

What's in wood? Fairies, they say – and dryads, tree nymphs cut off at the knees if you fell their forest. We light the woodstove on cool nights, and instantly I'm allergic.

What's in wood? we ask Charlie.

Fruiting bodies, he says. A growth, a fungus, that attacks the tree. He doesn't mention sprites of any kind.

Mornings, I walk up the logging trails splintering off the Diamond Road on either side of Diamond Farm. The logging roads are in better shape than the main arteries that the trucks tear up and leave to the taxpayers to fix, where your tires last a year, not the usual four, and where your car is in the shop for shock absorbers more often than not. No dryads, no deer on the logging roads. The song of a lone chainsaw drones down from the woods. Wouldn't it be something if I came across someone cutting up a body for disposal? *The Clue of the Solitary Chainsaw.* But I find only Pictou County: a garbage heap. Dirty diapers, squashed cans, milk cartons, a trike that the wheels had fallen off, with one rubber

grip still on the handlebars. The dump is littered with spent car-
tridges. On the night before hunting season opens, we're outside
when we see a white flash from the woods that circle the farm. A
rifle shot rings out behind it, honed on the clear night air. We phone
the Natural Resources people to complain about deer-jacking. The
guy up the road has little kids who play on the grounds, in the
woods, I say. Why am I lining up reasons for the authorities to
enforce the law? But nothing I say matters anyway. It's the cusp of
the season, and Natural Resources isn't sure whether we should
complain to them or the RCMP. We phone the RCMP, finding them
after working our way exhaustively through a catalogue of emergency numbers. By now, the deer jacked up on the hill in the woods
will be neatly, expertly dissected, packaged in freezer wrap, and
loaded in a truck. The RCMP thinks we might want to contact
Natural Resources: isn't it hunting season, sort of? Isn't deer-
jacking their problem?

  Isn't it illegal, in season or out?

  *Well sure, missus. But we got to decide who goes out. Whose
turn it is.*

⁓

To rate the "strangeness" of sightings, UFO enthusiasts use three
scales, named for the ufologists who devised them: Hynek, Berliner,
and Speiser. Likewise, there are the Hynek, Berliner, and Speiser
credibility scales, for rating the reliability of eyewitness accounts.
Dr. J. Allen Hynek, a professor of astronomy at Ohio State University and later chair of the astronomy department at Northwestern
in Illinois, served during the 1950s and 1960s as an expert consultant to Project Blue Book of the U.S. air force, determining whether

there were astronomical explanations for UFO sightings. How many witnesses? Hynek asked. If there is a pair or group of witnesses – hunters out under the evening sky, for example – what is their collective objectivity? How well can they gauge angular sizes, angular rates of speed? Just how good is their eyesight, anyway? What are their medical histories? What technical training have they had? What's their reputation in the community? For publicity-seeking? For veracity? What is their occupation and how much responsibility does it involve?

And what, he might have asked in Pictou County, is their level of sobriety?

Single witness cases, said Hynek, merited no more than quarter-scale credibility, but double or multiple witnesses – in Pictou, hunters, quad drivers in packs, guys revelling their way home from the bootlegger's – were more reliable. A TV camera documenting the event was best, said Speiser after him, but hunters were good too. They were used to spotting things.

Alas, for all its hunters and woodsmen, Pictou County's most famous UFO sighting involved only a lonely guy on his porch after a thunderstorm. The rest of the family was out for the evening; even the dog was somewhere else. He knows what he saw, however: a luminous oval hovering just short of the porch in the pitch night sky. It split into three discs before reconverging, pulling sudden, alarming focus, and scooting away. It was an event of "high strangeness," according to the Hynek, Berliner, and Speiser scales, and there was volition to it. That thing in the sky, the lonely guy knew, was *meant* for *him*.

According to the Speiser scale, here was an *S5, Highly Strange: Suggests Intelligent Guidance*. Events of high strangeness involve temporal doorways, light beams, discs, animal deaths, other beings, other worlds, abductions, body containers, souls of light. Events of high strangeness even involve the transfer of minds body to body, a form of abduction. The aliens take you away, they put you somewhere. Even into somebody else. Eventually, they give you back.

The view from the porch happened before we arrived. But *please*, B would say, *take us away anyway. Don't give us back.*

·~

Years ago when she was crossing her fields one December near the end of hunting season, Zelda felt a bullet fly by her ear. She felt a sting that took her breath away, felt the pressure and the pop of the mini sonic boom. That's what she remembers before she flattened herself to the snow and screamed. The RCMP found shells and cigarette butts where a pickup truck had stopped in a clearing in woods at the edge of the field, but nothing more, and right there is where a country investigation ends, when *no one got hurt, after all, just a little shook up*, and when you've no father or brother-in-law who's important or who's a lawyer or owns a car dealership in town or knows people in Halifax.

I tell B many stories about Zelda – we had twenty-five years together, after all – but not this one. The two of them had it out over the sale of the farm, exchanging insults, and he hasn't forgotten it. *And your point?* I'm afraid he'd say if he knew this story; *she's the Blair Zelda Project, after all.* For him it'll always be a bit of a joke, the way things ended, like something idiotic or unconscionable thing some politician did that makes the news, and he'll never get over her because he doesn't need to. But because

I do, there seem to be some things that are best only remembered, not revived.

⸱⤳

At the end of hunting season, weeks go by before we see deer again. But suddenly they're back, chowing down in our fields and jumping across the Diamond Road in front of us as we drive by, gunning it in pairs, threes, sometimes fives, looking for all the world like they've got to get to the Scotsburn Co-op in the village before the sale ends.

But where there's speed in the creatures, as if they're headed for something, there's sadness too, and for the same reason. When they look at us, as they always do, they look with huge, despondent eyes, liquid and black. We're into a hard winter this year, with snow already twice what it was the year before and some long bitter stretches when even the snow can't stay where it's driven by the wind.

Hey guys, I think at them in all seriousness through the car window, having long ago lost my belief in Santa Claus but never in animal telepathy, *Tony Nette in the Big Game Office won't be giving out as many licences next year, you can relax.* That's the part I send.

That's because this winter's bad enough now to take you down ahead of time. That's the part I keep to myself.

[F O U R]

Well-Wishers

L abour Day, arrival day. The rusted front end of a 1948 Dodge pickup is parked nose first in the brook that rounds the house, upended as if some local Jules Verne, years ago, had been in a great hurry to shoot himself wheels and all headlong into the centre of the earth. In our offer to purchase, we thought it reasonable to request it be removed, along with the rest of the antiques and flotsam that choked the house and the garage and the barns and the fields. *This Agreement is subject to the Sellers at their expense removing any equipment, vehicles, or other extraneous material not included in the purchase price, from the property before the closing date.*

Scarlet and Jo thought it unreasonable, and scratched it out.

B is furious and remains so until we take occupancy. And then things get worse.

The week we arrive is sultry and hot. We're camping, waiting for the moving van and our furniture. Charlie's loaned us a couple air mattresses and sleeping bags, and two lawn chairs with backs and seats of woven plastic lattice that we stick to in the heat. B has Viking blood; he hates the heat. He sets the chairs out by the brook where it's cool in the evenings. He sits there every night the week we arrive, above the truck, his feet on a picnic cooler, picking at a metallic screw in the seat rail of his chair.

"Hate that truck." He says it at least ten times a night, every night. He launches a bottle cap through the window on the driver's side.

"Mmmm," I say, also for the tenth time. I bend to the book in my lap, hope he'll go on to something else. I turn a few more pages. It's an account of two friends, physicians, and the life they try to share in urban El Paso while one grapples with a morphine addiction. It's full of traffic, freeways, parkades, office towers. The two friends are pressed; they keep impossible schedules. I read it with awe and an outsider's diffidence, as I would a book about French Polynesia or particle physics or the monoliths on Easter Island. Already, Vancouver seems very far away.

B has another beer, launches another bottle cap. *Hate that truck hate that truck hate that truck.* I've got a headache, and before long I crawl into my sleeping bag on the wide pine boards of the empty second floor. Distantly, I hear him on the phone.

I'm wakened around midnight by voices on the lawn beneath my window. I crawl out of my sleeping bag and look out. There's a wrecker pulled up to our door, and some sort of argument going on. I get a wet cloth for my head and wait. Voices rise and fall. An engine starts, guns, recedes down the driveway.

A door swings shut. B climbs the stairs.

"The auto club," he says, tipping back the end of a beer. "I told them I had a little accident and needed a pullout. They didn't buy it."

⋅⤙

Bill and Jim hook a line to the truck and pull it out with their tractor. It goes to rest in a garbage heap just inside the edge of our woods. There's plenty remaining on the fields to join it – long-forgotten sheds, outbuildings looking like they've taken a few meteor hits, an old oil tank and too many rusty oil drums to count. Half-rotted hay wagons on sunken tires, gnarled cultivators, rusted balers and manure spreaders. Scarlet and Jo had played at farming, buying all the latest toys only to let them rot in the fields. They bought their hay at the end of the summer.

Bill and Jim don't talk much about Scarlet and Jo. They're the women who sold us this place, who believed in keeping things, who had places for nothing that they kept and nothing in its place. They were big; they generated a lot of by-product, and when they moved they left it all behind. With shoulders like a linebacker, Josephine towered to six feet; and Scarlet, someone says, *had an arse as wide as my console TV*. Imagine the Giant McAskills as a same-sex couple; and now imagine them with a vacuuming phobia.

Bill and Jim tell us that Hughie Fortune down at the Branch has himself a little Cat, and that once we get a junk pile made by dragging all the Diamond rubbish into a single heap, he'll come and doze it all into the ground. For Bill and Jim, there's little more to it than that – rolling up our sleeves. Scarlet and Jo left a mess, that's all. They didn't pick up after themselves, that's all, and what can you do? Bill and Jim's reticence about Scarlet and Jo is the reticence country folk can have about discussing any of their neighbours. It's not because they were a same-sex couple. It seems like half the county here is lesbian, and Bill and Jim are nearly alone among the nation's aging, God-fearing men in finding them as natural as raccoons and foxes, or at least as common.

After Diamond, Scarlet and Jo move to rural Ontario to begin another landfill there, and we hear that they've adopted a little girl from an orphanage in China. Even for international adoptions, qualifying as adoptive parents requires that a social worker checks you out, along with your homemaking habits, in what's known as a home visit. Scarlet and Jo must have borrowed someone else's home the day their social worker came.

Scarlet and Jo can be found on the Internet, where you don't have to push aside much to find a place to sit. Their interests lie on-line, on feminist listserves that have to do with how easy it is for women to use the Internet. It isn't easy at all, apparently, but Scarlet and Jo are on the job. Assessing access, they call it, and they fester about it on Web sites and links and in newsgroups. They have papers posted on the Net; they've written books, or at least edited them, or at least written introductions; they've pulled down government grants. They're experts; they have degrees. Scarlet and Jo have quite a Net presence, but in life, in this community, for all their heft they had little presence at all other than what they commandeered. And they did commandeer. They were persuasive, assertive, louder than bullhorns. Few got in many words edgewise. Someone attended a community meeting they emceed; later that night she dreamed she was in her car, in a parking lot, with Scarlet and Jo coming at her. She backed up – right into a lamp post. It was either that, or stand up to them.

When they left Diamond, Scarlet and Jo weren't missed. *Only disconnect*. Their closest friends in the county didn't even know they were leaving until they were spotted at the Co-op in the village, collecting spare grocery cartons for packing.

Diamond Farm under Scarlet and Jo was like Noah's Ark mired on a muddy shoal, with all those pairs of everything coming and going and sludge tracked in everywhere. They had six of everything, though, not just two. Six cats. Six dogs, large ones. In the big barn, pigs the size of bathtubs that they hadn't had the heart to butcher. Not six of those, luckily, but a couple grown so large they couldn't stand, and when Scarlet and Jo left, they had to be destroyed by the vet and hauled away.

Scarlet and Jo left both barns packed about six feet high with hardened, petrifying manure. They'd lived at Diamond for eight years, and hadn't lifted a shovel.

The five basic steps to cutting a diamond: marking, cleaving, sawing, girdling, and faceting. In marking, a planner ponders the shape of a rough stone. Where are its imperfections? What's the direction of its cleavage? How to cut the rough to yield the greatest value? How to see what can be, in what's not? A flawless stone's one weakness is perfect cleavage. Hard as it is, a diamond will break easily if hit just so, and a skilled planner will dodge that blow. But for large stones he wants controlled cleavage, to produce smaller pieces. He makes his mark, grooves the stone, splits it, then sends it down for sawing. A diamond saw is a papery disk of phosphor bronze spinning at about four thousand revs a minute. This is faster than your car, which screams at that speed. The saw rim is charged with diamond dust, and uses more dust from the stone it's sanding. Sawing takes a while, four to eight hours to cut through a one-carat rough diamond. Then the stone is put on a lathe and girdled, or rounded, into a cone; after that, it's faceted. Eighteen principal facets go first on a brilliant cut diamond, but brilliant cut, the most popular cut, produces a round stone with fifty-eight facets. After the first facets are done, the stone goes on to the brillianteer, who places and polishes the other forty, using more tools charged with diamond dust. Great skill is the hallmark of the diamond-cutting team, but especially during these last stages. The facet angles must be exact for maximum brilliance, and precisely sized to preserve symmetry. A vast refractive power gives the diamond its extraordinary brilliance, and a properly cut gem returns more light to the eye. The diamond's fire comes from the separation of white light into the colours of its spectrum as it passes through the stone. The fifty-eight-facet brilliant is standard, but a "single cut" is a simple way of cutting that leaves a round stone with only those first eighteen facets. Any cut diamond other than the round brilliant or the single cut is called a fancy cut. Of these, there's the marquise, the emerald, the baguette, the heart (like the Hope), the pear (like Liz's), the kite, and the triangle. Smaller brilliants are called "melee," as are small diamonds used to embroider the settings for larger stones. The colour of a diamond is called its *water*. An especially fine diamond, one cut to yield the greatest value for its size, is called a diamond of the first water.

•

Diamond Farm is not a diamond of the first water. Nor the second, nor the third. Even though as part of the sale Scarlet and Jo have signed a disclosure statement saying that they are unaware of any problems with the well, we find that all they ever had was problems with the well. It takes us three months, four filters, a dozen tests, and close to $5,000 to get drinking water on tap.

This is how it starts. Charlie, who's been renovating with Ray before we arrive, leaves us the keys and a note. *Your water smells bad. Ray left you some from his place.* Sure enough, two large Coleman water jugs sit in the corner of the kitchen. Ray lets us keep them for months, and they become a staple in our lives – as do daily trips to the Green Hill spring half an hour away.

"I hear a lot of well complaints from the bench," Ted tells us. He's the circuit judge who hides out on his days off at his camp just down the road, overlooking the Diamond River. Wells are a tricky thing, *caveat emptor* and all that, says our lawyer. She's not impressed by the vendor signatures we have on our disclosure statement. We'd have to find people willing to testify that the vendors knew, she says. Not only that they knew, but that they *really* knew. We'd have to establish that it's a bad well problem. Not only that, but stacked up against all the other well problems up here, that it's a *really* bad well problem. It seems there's a certain allowable threshold to nondisclosure, to fibbing about your water quality.

"Oh, it's a *really* bad well problem," says B.

The average American uses nearly two thousand cubic metres of water annually, the average Dane just a ninth of that. And the average Norwegian? Mine stops showering except when company comes. The well water is so full of iron and sediment it turns everything red. We go through several shower curtain liners. The towels and the sheets will never be the same again – they look as if we've used them for wrapping garden tools or bloodied, murdered corpses. I get in it daily all the same, scrunching up my eyes and my mouth. I'll be a redhead in no time at all.

Winmill Plumbing and Building Supplies sits across the county from Diamond on the main road in River John, looking for all the world like a circus tent. It's squat, with fat vertical stripes of pale aqua and white. Watergate had its plumbers. We have Harold and Shirley Winmill, and Erwin.

Harold and Erwin plumb Diamond Farm while Charlie renovates, and when they've finished, you can't turn on a tap anywhere without reducing the water pressure to a trickle elsewhere. The drain pipes to the washer are stuck together with a lick and a promise, and our first wash extends to the bathroom floor. The pipes freeze throughout the house as soon as the temperature outside falls to zero. The hot water pipes freeze before the cold ones – because, Charlie explains, cold water pipes can sweat into your walls during the summer, "so they insulated those." Apparently it didn't occur to anyone to insulate them all.

Our first week of bilge water crests one dark and stormy Friday night, when suddenly nothing at all, of any colour, comes from the taps. The relays controlling the submersible well pump out in the south field by the road, five hundred feet from the house and nearly three hundred feet down, make the electro-mechanical equivalent of a death rattle. Harold establishes that the pump, hanging dead in the water at the end of a two-hundred-and-eighty-foot rope, is "no good." Three hours at emergency callout rates, another day's wait while a new pump is found, and a thousand bucks later, bilge flows again from the Diamond taps and flushes the Diamond john – which looks about the same after it's flushed as it did before. Harold and Erwin mutter to themselves. *Damn well weren't no good when it were drilled in '94, ain't no better now.*

Charlie hears that the pump's died. Scarlet and Jo would have put a few miles on it in their day, he tells us. They'd tried to flush out the well by running the pump continuously for days on end, finally giving up on it and resorting instead to a coliform-contaminated spring from the hills across the Diamond Road. Maybe we could get a backhoe up on the hill, dig out the spring at its source, put in a caisson, run a half-mile of new pipe under the road since the existing pipe's seventy years old and bound to go at any moment. Why don't we do that? Then we won't have to worry about the well any more.

We're stuck with worrying about the well: cleaning up the spring would probably be the biggest water distribution project in the history of northern Nova Scotia.

We get the well tested a lot, to see if we're making any progress or perhaps to make ourselves believe things could be worse. Perhaps they could be worse – we don't have arsenic, for example, and we don't have lead. In no time, we're on a first-name basis with the folks in the lab at the Agricultural College, who try to cheer us up with their accounts of what's in wells. Water sample after water sample from ours shows catastrophic levels of iron, and also more manganese than a body'd ever want, inside or out. Our water stinks of rotten eggs, and manganese is why. Manganese also helps to bring out the full blush of the sienna stain the iron leaves on everything. Bonus: we have coliform – not just in the spring line but in the well now too.

We call Harold every day. Two weeks and a set of towels goes by: plumbing is big business around here, with cottages in the summer and well problems all year-round, and Harold's busy. By now, I have Carol's dreadful news, and time gets strange. It wavers and speeds, then slows to a trickle. Sometimes it races, when I see her or hear from her and there's agitation, a flurry of doing or wishing or remembering or mourning. But most times it only seeps.

Eventually, Erwin calls back. For two grand, he'll sell us a green sand filter. It'll take out the iron and the manganese, but if we miss a day on the filter maintenance schedule, the potassium permanganate serving as its active ingredient will colour the water really red, not merely iron red – just its way to let us know, retroactively, that we'd drunk down a fatal dose and will soon be dead.

The time is out of joint, the centre cannot hold, the world is upside down. *Tell me about your worst pain* – that's my daily appeal to B. How can this be so bad when so much else has been worse? He falls for it, initially. He begins with memories of kidney stones. All his visions are nightmarish, but soon they have to do exclusively, predictably with water. There's the time he broke his ribs against a weather buoy in the North Atlantic, just off the southern tip of Greenland. *Damn thing quit sending its weather reports to the Sedco drill rig off St. John's, on the Flemish Cap. The rig used the reports for forecasts. I got sent out to knock the buoy back into shape. Asiak, it was called – can't believe I named it myself and then it set out to kill me. Asiak was the god of weather for the Greenland Innu, something like that. God of the damned, more like. The other buoy next to it was named Killick; my project partner, Bill Bacon, came up with that. I should've stuck with something homey, like he did. A killick's an anchor; more importantly, it's a bar in the basement of the Hotel Newfoundland in St. John's. So there we are, far away from the Hotel Newfoundland, on the supply boat the Zapata Toilet, the Zapata whatever – Zapata Marine was owned by George Bush, senior – you knew that, right? It was all downhill from there. Four days out; seas not too bad when we pulled in – maybe ten feet. Skipper nudged the boat up against the side of the buoy and there*

it was; I just stepped on to it. Hi Asiak, nice Asiak. I went below,
spent about a half-hour and found the batteries drained because the
radar transponder had locked ON. *Batteries weighed six thousand*
pounds so I wasn't about to replace them. When I got back up on
top, the boat was far away and the seas had gone to twenty feet.
They must have seen me because they came right over. Skipper came
on the loudhailer and yelled that he couldn't pull up against the
buoy because of the waves. He was going to cruise by slow – I'd
have to jump when I thought the time was right. He came within
five or six feet, seemed like twenty. I took a run and crashed into
the railing on the boat. I felt my ribs crack . . . Then the medic taped
me up . . . When B talks like this I'm lulled into other worlds of
terror and triumph and out of our own at Diamond. But the awful
nostalgia snaps him back to the present. He sits and stares. He
might have asked me the same thing, *What's your worst pain?* But
he's not the type to belabour the obvious.

We do more research, make more calls. B finds himself talking
to a Swede, of all people, someone who's in the industrial water-
quality business in the city and comes recommended. He steers us
toward an air-injected filter: not quite the brute-force approach of
green sand, but less likely to kill you. The air-injected filter arrives
but can't be installed, since the house is discovered to be fitted with
1¼-inch pipe rather than the standard 1½. Very little in the house
is standard. The shelves in the kitchen cupboards, for example, are
set too close together to accommodate even a regulation ketchup
bottle or a cereal box, and these litter our counters for want of a
place to be stored. As for the plumbing, the air-injector installer
promises to return with adapter fittings in a day or two, but the
water filter business is a busy one too. A few weeks later – another
shower curtain liner and another set of sheets – he arrives and

completes his job, then scrams before we can try it out. The air injector does nothing, and a subsequent test shows the iron is actually worse now than before. Air Injector Man says he has a new trick up his sleeve; he'll be back with it in a day or two. We know we have a couple weeks and perhaps a bedspread to kill, so while we wait we attack the coliform problem.

By now, we have enough experience with wells to know how to kill coliform – with bleach. The process is called shocking a well. You simply dump two or three gallons of bleach down the well, run it through the system, and wait. The first two jugs we use are No-Name. We're supposed to run the taps till we smell the bleach, then shut them off and let everything sit and disinfect overnight. B takes wrenches, a flashlight, and the bottles and disappears into the night, down the east field toward the well head. I count out five minutes, then run the kitchen taps. For nearly an hour. Shock a well right, and you'll smell chlorine at your taps almost immediately. We never did. What went wrong? We consult the municipality's official well inspector, who tells us there's a difference between *just bleach* and *real bleach* – Javex. The next night we try again. With three jugs of generic bleach and three more jugs of Javex in the well, we don't need to wait by the taps. We can go a mile down the road and smell the chlorine from Diamond.

It takes a full week to flush through. Coming in the front door you'd think you'd just entered the locker room of a public swimming pool. We have the cleanest bathroom fixtures I've seen in my life, and the whitest teeth.

Air Injector Man arrives back at the end of that week. He replaces the do-nothing filter with a new one, and adds a conventional salt-based water softener to the mix. The Diamond cellar is starting to look like the USS *Voyager*'s warp drive. The well water isn't red any more. Now, it's milky, and milky water is even less inviting to drink than red water. But I take heart, I steel myself, I cook spaghetti in it, I take one look at the spaghetti while it's boiling and I pitch the whole thing out.

We have a clay sediment problem, probably. Now that we've canvassed the great minds of the universe, that's all that anyone is left to come up with – sediment. Once we have it tested, we'll know for sure. The lab at the Agricultural College doesn't test for clay. On a visit to the city and the hospital, B drops me off at the palliative unit and carries on to the hospital lab.

A chemist considers our pickle jar. "Looks like clay," sure enough.

And to test and be certain?

"$180."

Then what?

"Then you'd know you've got clay in your water."

"But you just told me we have clay in the water."

"Yeah, but for $180 we write it down."

The Internet offers up several kinds of sediment filters. Even the local hardware store has one. B secures a $45 semi-transparent sexy blue plastic thing to one of the few remaining vacant valves in the cellar. It perks up the place, but the water still looks more like milk than water. The filter company has kindly provided a 1-800 number on the side of the filter box. We reach them in Toronto. They tell us to pull out the five-micron filter in the blue plastic thing, which came with it, and replace it with a one-micron filter, which didn't.

More trips to town. More ups and downs the cellar ladder. Still milky, though less so – as if Mr. Squeers of Dotheboys Hall has abandoned the milk at his Home for Boys and is now watering ours

·instead. We begin to appreciate how Neil Armstrong must have felt just before the *Eagle* landed.

A sub-micron filter will reduce our water pressure to just this side of nothing. But we can stick it under the kitchen sink, connect it to a dedicated faucet, and drink and fill the pasta pot from that. The side of the box of the sub-micron filter says it will take out typhoid, dysentery, cholera, giardia beaver fever, coliform, fecal coliform. It uses an impressive-sounding *silver-impregnated ceramic disinfection cartridge* not only to kill bacteria and like-sized particulate, but to trap it first.

For this filter, clay sediment will be a walk in the park.

·⤳

John Doulton made the first ceramic water filter in England, at the pottery he founded in 1815 at Lambreth on the banks of the Thames. His big break in the water-quality business came when Queen Victoria realized she had a problem with the palace plumbing, and commissioned a filter for the royal household. Hers was an agreeable marriage of technology and artistry, a gravity-fed stoneware sieve in a container of handcrafted earthenware. She was so pleased with it that she bestowed upon Doulton the right to stamp his work with the Royal Crest. John's son, Henry, introduced the Doulton carbon filter in 1862, the same year that Louis Pasteur's experiments with bacteria ended centuries of speculation that germs could generate spontaneously. In France, Pasteur invented his own filter, but Doulton's British filter was competitive, taken up by hospitals, labs, and water projects throughout the world. Even the early Doulton designs are still used today in Africa and the Middle East. Henry was knighted by Edward VII in 1901, and authorized to designate his work Royal Doulton, evermore.

Doulton's ceramic filters use diatomaceous earth, fossilized silt that's not earth at all, but seashells. My mother lays the same stuff down around her tender seedlings in hopes of offing the slugs in her garden. It's made up of tiny, ragged silicon casings left by the trillions of microscopic single-celled algae, called diatoms, that have inhabited the world's waters for the last one hundred and fifty million years. Diatoms are different from garden-variety algae – they weave themselves microscopic shells for protection and for locomotion. A diatom shell is like a perfect little colander, punched through with tiny holes in a pattern so regular that even the slightest design change usually signifies that a different species made it. When the diatoms died, their shells piled up on the bottoms of geological lakes and lagoons. When these dried up, they exposed rich deposits of diatomaceous "earth." Today there are more than fifteen hundred uses for the stuff, from milk and water filters to heat insulators to abrasives in toothpaste and polishers in nail polish. And slugs.

Ceramic filters can trap bacteria as small as .22 of a micron, or a hundred-thousandth of an inch. Filters having a pore size of .01 to .45 micron are said to be bacteriologically sterile, and .45 to 1 micron to be bacteriologically safe. The addition of oligodynamic silver to the porous outer shell of the filter controls regrowth of bacteria that get trapped on the walls or the pores of the filter. The silver releases positive ions when it contacts water. Bacteria take up these ions into their enzyme systems and find themselves neutralized by it.

Our silver ceramic filter screens for .3 micron-sized stuff, bacteriologically sterile. *Install in 30 minutes*, trumpets the instruction sheet.

Whoever has written it does not know Diamond Farm, or Harold, or Shirley, or Erwin, or Winmill Plumbing and Building Supplies.

To connect it to the cold water line under the sink that quickly, a hateful little contraption called a "self-penetrating saddle valve" is supplied with the sub-micron filter. You tighten it around the pipe, then you pierce the pipe with a kind of syringe that screws into it. This saves you having to cut the pipe, so long as Harold didn't get there before you did.

He did.

The saddle valve on our filter produces a dribble of water. If we start filling a drinking glass at dawn, we can have it with dinner. Clearly, the saddle valve has to go, in favour of a more standard tee connector. But Harold's left his mark on the under-sink plumbing, without a translation. WiwaR to WoduridaR.

On a display board at Central Supply in the town, B finds what looks like identical pipe to what's under our sink. He asks for a tee fitting to suit it, and is told that the pipe in question is a special product intended for sub-floor heating. When you're rich, you run the stuff under the floor in your rec room, and then the kids can sit and watch TV in their sock feet all year round. No, Central Supply doesn't have any tee connectors for that kind of pipe, and B shouldn't be using that stuff for plumbing in any case.

Humbled, B retreats, reconsiders. It's Harold's pipe. Harold must have fittings.

In River John under his aqua-and-white-striped Big Top, however, Harold doesn't know any more what kind of pipe went under our sink all those months ago: "red and blue rolls of the stuff come in the front door, and we install it." He hands B a crimper as long as his arm, some crimping rings, something that looks vaguely like a tee connector. The crimper is a rusty, wrenchlike affair that Fred Flintstone might use in his Bedrock kitchen to help Wilma bone pterodactyl for dinner. Harold wants it back before closing, along with any leftover crimp rings. Who knows what he's having tonight?

We must proceed as if we can make a difference, even if we think we can't. Back at Diamond, B discovers that mere mortals don't install crimp ring fittings; it requires a kind of horsepower and perhaps some black magic known only to Harold and Erwin. But he's past the point of no return – he's hacked off the cold water pipe under the sink, and we're out of water till the job's complete. A fast run into town. This time, Home Hardware has what we need, a tee connector with compression fittings. Back at Diamond, getting the compression fittings onto Harold's mystery pipe slices up B's fingertips. Two hours of fiddling and a few Band-Aids later, we have lift off, we have drinking water. A half an hour up to the Big Top and a half an hour back: B returns to Harold his medieval instruments of torture. Back home finally, he cracks open a bottle of Scotch, pours himself half a tall glass, and tops it with water from the new tap.

It's been three months, five thousand bucks. And all it took was an upgraded warp drive in the cellar.

·‿

North Americans take so many painkillers that analgesic residues end up in our drinking water. But not at Diamond, not in its well. No painkillers here; none anywhere. I'm driving in the ambulance with Brian and Dave. As I look back now, it's hard to know whether we were coming or going – coming home from the hospital after a crisis, or going back because of one. Does it matter any more? Does the timetable matter when we all know how it ends?

I'm up front, sitting in the passenger seat amidst clipboards and papers and phones and gadgets and cables and flashlights and altogether more gear than is in even the Diamond cellar, and it's not where I want to be. Brian and Dave won't let me sit with her in the back, it's against regulations. They don't have insurance.

I have insurance, I hear her whisper. *Pffft.*

I've been by her side, and I don't want to be removed now. I've been keeping up with her, step for step, talking to her. Not about our new place, though – the nightmares, the cat, the well, the wind, the faithlessness. You can't talk trivia to a best friend dying. *Trivia*: from the Latin *tri* + *via*, three streets. At any intersection of three streets in ancient Rome, the Romans threw up a sort of kiosk where they posted ancillary information, who knows about what? The annual pork chop barbecue at the Capitol. *Great Mouser Free to Good Home. Claudia's Kitchen Table Repair. Thumbscrewing: Cheap. Phone Kevin in Marina Del Rey.* You might be interested in what was at your crossing; you might not; and so it was trivia. Carol is interested in everything at her crossing, and in nothing; where she's bound, she needs no signposts. But she is unambiguous about my crossing, downright uninterested. As am I myself, truth be told. I simply use it to fill the time I have. *I could give all to Time except – except What I myself have held.* I plaster my kiosk with the handbills I'm given; it fills the space. There's that staple of therapy these days about not sweating the small stuff. *It's all small stuff*, the therapists say. *Ask yourself, will it matter in a year?* For me, it's a fearful notion, it's harder than stone: none of it will matter in a year, only what I've lost. And that will matter, and never stop.

I've been by her side, holding on to her for dear life as they wheel her around, as I argue with Brian and Dave. She's wearing the plush navy robe she bought during the nightie shopping spree, and a navy beret pulled down over her ears. "Here, I'll sign a waiver," I say. I don't like to be made to disconnect our hands. It doesn't seem to bode well. "I'll absolve you of responsibility. I need to stay right next to her."

Brian and Dave have heard it before. "We don't have anything for you to sign," Brian says, pulling his pockets inside out as if he might normally keep his files and charts there.

Brian doesn't always drive. He and Dave take turns. They work with a third guy, a skinny kid who doesn't get introduced. He's a trainee, and they make him push the stretcher. It's an arduous job; maybe that's why he's so thin. When they're on the ground they move Carol at a clip, as if they're on commission, not salary, and the more transports they make, the more their take-home pay.

Brian is relatively new at being a paramedic, just two years now. He's chewing gum next to me, talking non-stop. It's hard to talk to Carol over his chatter. I don't worry about missing what she might be saying back. These days, she doesn't speak much.

Dave's been at it for ten years, Brian says.

"Six," Dave corrects him from the back. "It just feels like ten."

"Feels like ten to me, and I've only been here two!" Brian snorts, pleased with his unfathomable little joke. I hope Carol can't hear this, back there on her stretcher, or if she can that she has the sense not to try to keep up. How is it for her, I wonder, to have her last few days on earth filled with the likes of Brian and Dave?

Once we were strapped in for this trip, Carol in the back and me in the front, Brian didn't open the driver's door to get in. He leapt straight up and jumped through the window. An ambulance is a big machine. It was an impressive leap. *Dukes of Hazzard,*" he said, settling down in his seat, pleased with himself.

"Carol," I called over my shoulder to the back of the van. "We've got a driver out of a Hollywood movie."

"*Dukes of Hazzard*," he said again, with a tone to his voice. It was a correction. He wanted me to get it right. He wears cool shades. His cropped hair is gelled into a profusion of small spikes, as if a box of carpet tacks has spilled onto his head and stuck there. His wristwatch has a fabric band stamped with happy faces in bright yellow and bubble-gum pink. The worst part of the job, he tells me, is driving sirens and lights.

I'm surprised – I'd think it would be the sadness, perhaps the gore of car accidents, the inevitable deaths.

"Nah," he says. "Sirens and lights. Man, when you gotta go on sirens, people don't even pull over. They don't respect 'em."

"They disrespect 'em," Dave echoes from the back.

Brian doesn't see a lot of DOAs anyway. When he does, that's the second worst part of his job, talking to the relatives. He makes Dave do it whenever he can.

I look at him sideways, at the jaws working the gum, the hand tapping the steering wheel to some rap only he can hear. I can't imagine this pimply kid telling me my mother's passed on. Would he even know enough to take off his shades and swallow his gum? *Passed on.* That's what he'd say. They don't even say *passed away* any more.

"What did you think of Brian and Dave?" I ask her when they've screeched to a stop, deposited us, wheeled her around a bit, and gone.

"Waste of skin," she says.

I'm alarmed. It'd been a favourite expression of my angry, alcoholic ex-husband, and I'd never heard her repeat it, or anything like it. "Carol. Sweetie. They weren't that bad. They were good for a laugh. You've lost your sense of humour."

She fixes her wide, black eyes on me. "I've lost everything."

It's probably the most matter-of-fact thing I've ever heard her say, sick or well, just three words, and I feel as though some great splinter of ice has reached down my throat into my chest and hacked out a piece of my heart. It's so obviously, patently true, so staring-you-in-the-face true, and yet I hadn't seen it till she said it. How is it that all this time I've been wanting her to be the same as ever, hoping she'd jive and spar and keep up with me as usual? Shame jumps in me like flames. How else have I betrayed her, in her hour of need? She still has her blue beret jammed down over her ears and I realize suddenly, guiltily, that I've been glad of that hat because it hides the hair under it that is by now so awful. What if it's hot, scratchy on her poor dying head? It's as if I've been wanting her damage covered up for my benefit, not hers. I catch my breath, I can't talk. There's two of us, now, who can't talk.

⤙

Though her whole story lies ahead of her, Naomi is already a widow by the time we find her in the Old Testament Book of Ruth. Her husband is gone; her two sons have died as well. Time for you to leave, she tells her sons' widows, her daughters-in-law Orpah and Ruth. Time for you to return to your own homelands and your own families.

Orpah kisses her mother-in-law, packs and goes; but Ruth cleaves to Naomi. *Intreat me not to leave thee*, she says,

> *or to return from following after thee: for whither thou goest, I will go; and where thou lodgest, I will lodge: thy people shall be my people, and thy God my God: Where thou diest, I will*

die, and there will I be buried: the Lord do so to me, and more
also, if ought but death part thee and me.

I could not have said it so well, but it was what I had in mind
when I came home, when I returned to the bosom of my friends.

And when I arrived, there was nothing here.

⋅➤

Nights when I cry, I get up and sit under the window. With a bit
of a moon I can just make out the south field under the grip of
darkness. To keep an eye on me, B rolls his pillow under his neck
to prop up his head, and puts on his glasses. It's a strange thing
to see, a shadow in bed across the room wearing glasses, but it's
like him.

Tonight the moon is full, but so far overhead at this hour that
it's out of sight through the windows. I strain to see it. I stand up
on the sofa and twist my head around. *The moon*, I say to the
glasses in bed across the room. *I think it's full, but I can't see it.*

He gets out of bed, runs down the stairs, and opens the front
door. Standing in the buff on the porch, he can just see it far overhead, hanging over the peak of the roof. *It's full as they come*, he
reports back. It's seventeen below, he hasn't got a stitch on, but
he's found me my moon. When I go back to bed I walk on the cool
loonies and quarters that have fallen onto the carpet from the
pocket of his jeans. With an angel in your corner it can be like the
streets of heaven here, paved with gold.

Cold blows down the hills. Every morning, B brings me coffee
and a weather report. *It's minus ten, windy. I got up and put the*
quilt on you in the night. The fire was way down to embers, but

I've got it going now. On balmier mornings, there's frequently also a duck report: *five of them busted out of the barn overnight and were there under the window at five a.m., agitating for the release of the other three. How can you sleep through this stuff?*

·—

My B is like Microsoft Bob, the program Microsoft designed a few years ago to help make computers friendlier, more accessible to everyone in the home including the kids. It had big, affable signs and brightly coloured buttons. It promised to organize you with a Microsoft Calendar and a Microsoft Address Book, to keep track of your bills on Checkbook, to help you stay in touch with natty-looking letters from Letter Writer. You were even promised personalized help from Bob's Personal Guides. Bob would produce To Do lists for every member of the household, reminding them of jobs recorded in his Household Manager. Bob would keep birthday and anniversary dates in his Address Book, and remind you when a special day was coming up. You could also choose from among ten or more of Bob's Friends to help you when and where you needed it. They could even learn how you liked to work so that they wouldn't bother you with help you didn't need or want.

I'm not making any of this up. Microsoft Bob never made it past version 1.0, but he lives on today in the interface behind the talking, dancing, sodding paper clip that offers to help you write letters and find things when you use Microsoft Office. Paper Clip Bob.

But the more my B tries to ground me, the more I feel lost. The house and everything in it continues to reel between *falling apart* and *getting fixed*. One day the coffee grinder goes; next day, the kettle. The clocks keep stopping. Okay, we ask each other, who's got the lava rock?

⌣

Bill and Jim offer to fell the big dead elm in the east meadow, before it blows down in a wind and takes out the house. They drive their half-ton into the middle of the field, tie a line to its back bumper, and throw the end of the line over a high branch. Bill's wiry; he shimmies up the tree like a teenager and secures the line. They move the truck farther into the field and put some tension on the rope, so that when the tree comes down it will fall toward the truck and away from the house.

We watch these preparations from the window. I keep looking at the size of the tree; I keep looking at the size of the truck. *I know how this would turn out in Monty Python,* I say to B, but I'm only half right. With their chainsaws, they notch the tree on the wrong side, toward the house, and cut it on the other, and when it falls, it falls straight into the roof. The line lets go, the truck shimmies and staggers in the field. The dishes rattle in the antique hutch. We stare at the roof, all of us, open-mouthed.

I'm trapped in Brigadoon now, unable to leave without bringing the place down around my head. Fiona Campbell's sister, Jean, is smack in the middle of getting married the day Tommy Albright and Jeff Douglas stumble into town. Tommy and Jeff join the wedding festivities, but petulant nogoodnik Harry Beaton doesn't – he glowers from the sidelines. Harry's an earlier suitor, whom Jean has jilted. He's so despondent he'll leave Brigadoon, he says: he doesn't care what happens now that he's lost Jean.

I'm like Harry; I'm threatening. B is getting to know the neighbours, shaking his head at the foibles of the house. *It's a great life
if you don't weaken* – he likes to say that, just because he doesn't
really believe he is weakening. He thinks he'll make it; scratched
and torn, he'll nonetheless prevail. It doesn't occur to him that he
might fail. For me, it doesn't occur to me that I won't. B's making
his peace with the place, and soon he'll be sampling the sweets
from the wedding reception. But I'm threatening.

People with Alzheimer's wander so frequently at night that
there's a name for it. Moonlighting, it's called. They get up in the
night to go to the bathroom and think, *Wow, where am I? Whose
bathroom is this, anyway? Who picked that wallpaper? What a
place to put the light switch. Who could ever find it there?*

Gosh, it's late, they must think. *Better get home quick.* And so
they dress, rush down the stairs, head for the door.

·ᴗ

We hike up an old logging trail to an Addams Family house known
locally as the old Gratton place. The path isn't really a logging trail
at all, but an overgrown driveway that climbs the hill for at least a
mile before it opens onto a broad green lea, overhung today with
a big pewter sky. A few clouds scud by above us, through the tree-
tops. B holds branches back while I pass. When we emerge into the
clearing we both stamp our feet, as if the old house extends its
threshold right to our boots.

The building is ramshackle, with the frame of a 1940s car
melting into the ground on the far side. The floors and the walls
are funnelling together, tipped inward and sinking as if someone's

pulled a plug in the centre hallway so that the house can drain away. There's exquisite scrollwork carved into the window mouldings, badly weathered but beautiful still. What was it like for the Grattons to live here into the 1960s with no power, no plumbing? Why did they endure an otherwise spartan life but care so much about their trim?

I walk the perimeter of the house while B waits. Again I walk it, and again. Will weaving a circle around it make it give up its secrets? It's a mild December day. Only a few patches of snow remain from a recent storm, filling in the dips in the ground. It seems we can walk west through the evergreens and meet up with the Sutherland Road, near the gates to the old Diamond Cemetery, so we strike out. But we walk for half an hour and never come to it. By now the shadows are long, and we turn around and go back the way we came. It's better than getting lost.

And if we were lost?

"We'd read our reference points from the sun," B says lazily.

"We'd what?"

"Well, I would. You'd wait."

"I'd be bloody cold, waiting."

"I'd give you my jacket."

"Then you'd be bloody cold."

"No I wouldn't; I'd get us out of here in no time."

"And if you couldn't? If you couldn't read our reference points?"

"Then we'd deserve to die."

"Speak for yourself."

He could do it, though; these are the kind of things he knows. So often it seems to me that he stretches the plastic wrap of literalness and calculators and science facts over the real blood and guts of life and skates away on it, but most of what he knows can be plenty useful in a pinch. It's an arcane science, finding your way. The points of the compass aren't even straightforward.

There's true north, for example, and then there's magnetic north.

A compass is magnetic; responding to the pulls of the giant magnet earth, it points to magnetic north. As the geographical end of an imaginary axis through the planet on which it spins once every twenty-four hours to make a day, true north is the geographical north pole. These poles are not in the same place, and the difference between them, called *declination*, depends on where you are.

These days, the magnetic north pole is located between Alert and Resolute Bay in the Arctic, straight north of Winnipeg by about two thousand miles. If you happen to be in Winnipeg looking north, the geographic pole and the magnetic pole are in line, so there'll be no difference, no declination. If you're in Halifax, the magnetic pole looks like it's about twenty-one degrees to the left of true north. If you're in Vancouver, magnetic north seems to be to the right. Like most things in life, it's all a matter of perspective.

The magnetic pole is on Ellef Ringnes Island by Alert, for now. The geographic pole never moves – it's located in the middle of the vast Arctic ocean where the chill black waters, under their great thickness of ice, are nearly fourteen thousand feet deep. But the magnetic pole does move, circling the geographic pole once every nine hundred and fifty years. The earth probably owes its magnetic charge to the flow of molten iron at its core. Because the flow pattern drifts over time, the position of the magnetic poles changes too. A quarter of a century ago, the magnetic pole was on Bathurst Island in Canada's north, about two hundred miles east of where it is now. It's leaving the country soon, on its long, millennial circle around the globe.

There's actually another north pole, too, says B. Geomagnetic north, currently on the northwest coast of Greenland, is where the earth's magnetic fields converge. Geomagnetic north and magnetic north aren't the same. The two are about four hundred and fifty miles apart, separated by Ellesmere Island. B's in his counting-the-days-at-Brigadoon, Microsoft Bob mode; soon he'll be pulling out his calculator. But I can't deal with a pole in Greenland. As it is, two norths seem far too many.

Maps are laid out in terms of true, geographic north. The farther north you go, the worse the discrepancy between it and magnetic north, the greater the declination. If you're in Resolute Bay and someone says "walk north from here," don't rely on your compass – it will point you not north at all, but west. If you're halfway between Resolute Bay and the North Pole, your compass will actually point you south.

Given all this, my question is, how do you know when you're halfway between Resolute Bay and the North Pole to begin with, if your compass won't point you there? Street signs?

The sign at the Durham crossroads blew off its post in an early-autumn windstorm. No one's ever replaced it. It used to point to the village of Scotsburn and then farther west, down the 256 to Diamond. Undressed, the white post with its crossbar stands there dumbly today at the end of the Durham Hills Road, looking like it's been transported out of Flanders Fields or Arlington Cemetery. Add to that the scarcity of signs to Diamond on the 256 itself, and you come up lost. If you haven't been here before or if you don't have people to meet you, there's no way to know where you are.

Nova Scotia is the lost-person capital of North America. More people *per capita* get lost in woods here than anywhere else – probably because we have so much woods to get lost in.

Men and women get lost differently, it seems, and have different navigational styles for getting themselves found. Women seem
to follow a route in finding their way, depending on landmarks as
they appear in a sequence. *There's the market, then that mailbox
on the corner with the side bashed in where some car ran into it. I
turn at the next light.* Men have a survey style of navigating
instead, where they overview a block of geography to know where
they are. My Microsoft Bob is like this. He can see a map of the
whole of northern Nova Scotia in his mind, and without thinking
about it can orient himself to compass points. I took him outside
once and made him close his eyes tight, then I spun him around
three times.

"Now," I said, "open your eyes and quick as you can tell me
which direction you're facing." Not that I would have known
whether he was right.

He opened his eyes. "D," he said mournfully. "I know where
we are. Don't you believe me?"

Men and women even disagree about whether they *are* lost. A
woman will say *let's stop and ask*, fearing the worst; but to the
bitter end, a man will know where he's going. That may be too
bad, because there are things lost people do to protect themselves
or to find their way out which they don't do if they don't know
they're lost. Hunters may be the exception to the male pride rule.
When they seem to be lost they're usually not, and most walk out
by morning.

Whatever you do or don't do if you're lost in the woods, an
absolute failure of spatial orientation will eventually overtake you.
It's called wood shock, and for many people it's the beginning of
the end. Entranced, people in wood shock have walked right past
the searchers looking for them. Some even retreat, hide, run deeper

into the woods. Many people who are grievously lost become convinced they're going the right way. By walking, the lost person complicates his own search by enlarging the search area.

"That's right," B agrees.

"But you said if you were lost, you'd walk until you walked out."

"Well, I'd know where I was going. It wouldn't make any sense then to do anything but walk out."

I wring my hands. "If you knew where you were going, you wouldn't be lost, then, would you? It just goes to show. You're one of those men who'll always disagree that he's lost."

There's a pause. He smiles broadly. "Well, what can I tell you. It's how the Fakawi tribe got their name. They got up every morning and said *where the Fakawi*."

When hunters do get lost, they've been concentrating on what they're tracking rather than on where they are. They push themselves in hope of the prize, and they push the limits of the day too. A hunter's sundown is later than sundown for the rest of us. Weather's a factor in their disorientation only occasionally; darkness is responsible more often. Hunters are more detectable than other lost people, though, because of those vests and caps they wear the sickening colour of the orangeade at the Aberdeen Mall.

Seasoned hikers and climbers tend to be well-equipped and self-sufficient. So long as they're unhurt, when they get lost they're not in as much danger as the rest of us. The leading cause of accident for climbers, by far, is slipping and falling. Runners-up are falling objects and ego, where the climber's reach has exceeded his grasp. Only a few more climbing accidents happen on rock than on snow, but the accident rate going up an incline is nearly double what it is coming down. When a climber is overdue it's often because of an accident, as it is with lost fishermen, who tend to be well-oriented otherwise. Such veterans of the outdoors don't get lost so much as they meet fate.

Small children act a lot like people with Alzheimer's when they're lost. They usually won't respond to searchers calling their names. They've been taught not to talk to strangers, after all. The elderly person may not respond either, out of deafness or disorientation. Both tend to walk till they're stopped by something – some obstacle in the landscape, or fatigue. They usually travel downhill, and not very far – at most, a quarter-mile from where they started. Neither the young child nor the adult has any idea he's lost.

Alzheimer's sufferers who get lost are what search-and-rescue people call *walkaways*. That's what they call missing despondents too. Despondents generally maintain that they haven't been lost at all; they've merely been getting away to think. They're usually found readily, so long as you look in secluded spots, open spaces surrounded by trees, always some distance from trails. Berry pickers, rock hounds, nature photographers – all these, on the other hand, are poor survival risks. They're unprepared, unfit, underclothed, and while they intend to stay in one place, in their anxiety they wander and make things worse.

Which is petulant Harry Beaton, in *Brigadoon*? In his anxiety, he wants to wander and make things worse. Which am I, I wonder? I'm a despondent half the time, out here in my neck of the woods where everyone's suddenly disappeared, where my familiars have departed without a word of warning. But I'd never deny that I'm lost. I'm bloody lost, no question. I'd throw myself on my rescuers: *Thank God you're finally here, I've been lost without you.*

But like those berry-pickers I'm unprepared too. It's been a total shock, the cold and the confusion, and here I am without even a sweater.

Psychologists have researched how people learn to find their way. They've studied children to see how they develop an understanding for permanent landmarks. That's an important piece of the puzzle, because to find your way by landmarks, you have to realize that environmental cues are permanent, not arbitrary.

Older children have learned this, and when they're lost they behave differently from little kids. In older children, the neurosis of adulthood has begun to set in. These kids often get lost because they want to – they run away from home out of anger or to avoid it, or to get attention. They may not answer searchers until they get cold or hungry, and darkness usually brings them out of their hiding places. Their navigational sense is nearly as good as an adult's, and when they're truly lost they taste fear like an adult does too, only worse. They're lonelier, they feel more helpless.

Not lonelier than me, though, not more helpless than me. I may be an adult, but nobody could feel as lonely and as helpless as me. I was not always as you see me now.

When we were kids making that all-day drive in the Vauxhall, to dentists and doctors in the city and then home again, my mother stopped one evening on the road to get a snack. It was unlike her, to give in to the lure of a restaurant, and unlike me too, that I slept through it in the back seat. She and my sister went in and got a window seat. She wanted to keep an eye on me in the car. While she decided to leave me there rather than wake me up, she wanted to be sure that if I did wake she'd see me, and come running out to reassure me. I didn't wake, but somehow this non-memory feels to me as if I did, as if I awakened into dark nothingness and screamed and screamed and never saw them again, my mother and my sister, when all the time they were eating pie behind the plate-glass front window of a diner, a few yards' declination from my head. *Your*

life will abandon you like that. It will just up and go, that's the
truth of the story that somehow latched on to me as a kid, *and take
the pie too.*

In me, an invincible winter. But to hear myself pine now, to
know that other people around here also get lost at an alarming
rate, that rescue is possible and there's a science to it, to know that
there's *declination*, that everything's a matter of perspective, and
that sooner or later we all have to sort out what's permanent and
what's not – something about it all makes me think I might have
that again one day, a sign, a way out, the albatross removed from
round my neck, a great, possessing friendship or two.

·⤳

*The hangman bound her hands, cut her hair, and placed her
on the ladder. He threw alcohol over her head and set fire to it
so as to burn her hair to the roots.*

*Once again he placed her thumbs and big toes in the vise,
and left her in this agony on the torture stool from ten a.m. to
one p.m., while the hangman and the court officials went out
to get a bite to eat.*

– account of the torture of a woman accused of witchcraft
at Prossneck, Germany, in 1629, from Wilhelm Pressel, *Hexen
und Hexmeister* (1860)

Her eyes are bruised, her skin leprosy white like Life-in-Death, the
nightmare woman who dices for the life of the Ancient Mariner.
She's sitting, but her head is hardly raised from the pillow. She
looks like someone who's been drinking all night, out of focus and
trying hard to dial herself back in.

She's back here now in the hospital after a session at home, where she had control of her drugs. She'd phoned my mother, the nurse who knows drugs, and rhymed off all the labels of all the bottles in her cookie tin. *Enough to kill me?* she'd rasped into the phone. *Which? How many? Please. Tell me, please. No one will help. Don't worry. I'll stay on the phone once it's done, while I fade*, said the first Mrs. Wilcox feebly. *Won't just go. What. Order. Help. Me.* I searched the Web for the Hemlock Society, I called a friend with AIDS in Toronto who wouldn't talk to me about suicide or doctors who might help because just then he was on the upswing, thinking positive, and by the time I got to her with information the crisis had passed. On the phone to my mother, she only says again, *Can you stand three girls? Can you adopt me?*

I already have, my mother says.

No one talks about suicide again. We should have.

Now, she asks me where I've been. When I come to see her, she always asks me that. I dread the question; I'm guilty that I've been anywhere at all. I wonder what she thinks about her haunts and her vistas now, the park and the city duck pond where she walked the dog so faithfully, the favourite greenhouse on Highway 7, the Second Cup in the mall and the Chinese place nearby with the good hot and sour . . . all the other places she used to go without a second thought, without a look back. I wonder if she feels lost. She's the only one of us now beyond hope of rescue. If she were a child, she'd crawl under a picnic table, an overhanging rock, and go to sleep. Because she's an adult, the hospital won't let her.

"Where?" she asks me again.

"Chapters."

"Chapters?"

"The bookstore."

"Right. Thought your membership expired."

"Membership?"

"Uh huh." A fleeting movement – a pick at the sheet with a fingertip. She's self-conscious; she knows she's getting something wrong. *I couldn't stand to have my mind go,* she said when she was diagnosed. *It's what I fear the most.*

Me, it's what I'd want the most, to stumble away into some sort of black, and I told her that.

Really? she said. Not me.

You're brave, I said.

Really? she said.

"Costco," she says now, with effort.

I scramble up to bat. I don't want her to think for a minute that she's been incomprehensible. "Right, we're stopping there on our way out of the city, if we have time. And yes, we'll have to renew our membership."

But that's not what we do on our way out. I can't face Costco. Carol and I used to go there for the cheese, great wedges and blocks of Jarlsberg and Edam and pots of creamy blue, for premium white cheddar so dry it crumbled, and all for next to nothing.

These days, I don't care if I never see cheese again. B and I drive to her house instead, and there we put her garden to bed, digging up her dahlias and glads to pass to her friends for next year. It's late November. We've brought pails, gardening gloves, shears, garden forks and spades, labels for the tubers, ties for the labels, permanent markers for the ties.

Permanent markers? the clerk has said to me at the greenhouse. *You want permanent markers? Have you ever found one that truly is?* He's young in his apron, waving his garden hose like a maestro;

he smirks at the little japes of life that sit on my head with the weight of grinding stones.

We've brought our Wal-Mart boots to Carol's, because we have to wade through this too. Digging dahlias is always a hard job, since you get soaked at it and since you're forever doing it in the cold, after several killing frosts. You can't do it earlier. Everything has to have hardened off first.

In Carol's garden, the wind whistles down the paths and aches inside my ears. It's painful, pulling up things she'd planted in the spring before we knew any of this. It's painful chopping down the stalks, seeing the tags and markers she'd written in that classic hand, seeing the design she'd thought out and worked into the ground. *Which? How many? Tell me, please. What. Order.* In the time it's taken for these hunks of last year's dried root to plump up, put out feeders, throw up stalks, and unfurl leaves and bloom again, her life has ground to an end. It was there in the spring, hale fellow well met, and no one thought otherwise: now, in mere months, it's nearly gone. The mystery of it is unfathomable. It stuns me. Someone is speaking to me, someone is calling across the frosty lawn; there is knowledge here, and I can't make out a word. I'm like someone having a stroke, impenetrable and at the same time flooded with something terrible I can't name.

I look around and around her lawn, her garden, the shingles and trim of her house. White on ochre. Ochre on white. Ochre, white. White white white, and in the earth all the drained, wet colours of November. It all turns around me, a dreary mottling with the core blasted out, and I can't see how to get on with this job. How could she have been here in spring, not now? B just looks at me blankly. Well, she's dying, he says by way of explanation, and he shuffles his feet in his Wal-Mart boots. Three years earlier I gave her these plants. We'd sold our house and were packing for Vancouver, and I dug up my dahlia beds and asked her to grow them for me while I was away, the Esthers and the Sneezies and the Gerrie Hoeks, the Alfred Grilles, and the Popular Guests. I hosed down the tubers and laid them out to dry in the sun, then bundled the best of them into a large onion bag of orange netting. Here they are again now, a chain of evidence of our years together. They were meant to multiply and be divided between us, whenever I made it back and had my own garden again.

And now the chain is broken, one of us is stopped in time and won't go on, and the other's left holding the bag.

It's one of the last times I'll be at her house, I know that, but it's too cold to cry. Certainly it's the last time I'll be puttering where once we puttered side by side, digging in the dirt: impatiens, phlox, nicotiana, bee balm, geraniums, ranunculus. Now it's B by my side, digging the dahlias with me stalk for stalk, without knowing or caring much what a dahlia is.

Dinner plates, I tell him, leaning on my garden fork, curving my hands and holding them a foot part. *Some of the blooms are that big and that's what they're called.*

No, he says, as if he couldn't be more charmed.

We stop at a pay phone as we leave the city. She's letting the hospital switchboard put through her calls again, for today, at least. She answers after several rings, when I'm about to hang up. "Sweetie. We had time so we stopped by your house and did your garden. I've got the dahlia tubers all hosed down and in boxes in the back of the car. I've got the glad corms too. I'll put everything in sulphur and peat when I get home."

"Mmmmmmm." She's roused herself from sleep and drugs,

but her relief is palpable. As the cold encroaches she's been worry-ing about the garden. Even though she has no future she can still imagine one for her plants.

"We raked all the beds over. Hung up the hose. Looks good as new."

"God bless you." A pause, a cough. "Where you now?"

"Costco. We're at Costco."

"Have to renew your membership."

·ᴖ

Anyone who's spent more than a minute or two on the Prairies will tell you that a sump pump in the basement is simply *de rigueur*. You have a sump pump, or you have an indoor swimming pool. Your choice.

B has lived on the Prairies. Diamond didn't have a pump until he insisted on it, but it did have a history of spontaneous swim-ming pools.

In November, a sudden storm leaves two feet of snow in our fields. Then a sudden thaw melts it all overnight – straight into our cellar. Water pours in with enough force to pop the sump pump liner out of its hole and topple the pump on its side, where it pumps nothing and in no time will short out.

It's Smike who sounds the alarm and rouses B from bed. He's wailing – not because of the cataract below, pouring into the cellar, but because he's been locked in the bathroom for the night for wailing. B is on his way to throttle him when he decides to check the basement. He stands knee deep in icy melt from two in the morning until four, holding the pump upright. Finally it pumps out enough of the flood that along with its liner it can be forced back into its hole. By the end of the next day he's been to the hardware store in town and grounded the thing with spikes. He covers the top of the pump liner with a huge log for good measure.

While B stands for those two hours in the melt, I lie in bed a floor above and hear nothing. If he's doing something about Smike, or about the storm, he's doing it quietly. Around three in the morning I decide *no he's not, he's been electrocuted*, and I get out of bed and go downstairs. I need to see how hard it's going to be to drag his body up the ladder from the cellar, to see whether or not I'm going to have to call 911 and wait in a queue on a black night like this, till someone comes.

And then he hears me. He calls me to bring him a pair of gloves. I go to the kitchen and hunt under the sink for rubber gloves; half asleep, I have some vague idea they'll keep him from being electrocuted since he hasn't been after all. Not so far, anyway.

What he really wants, of course, is work gloves. Frostbite is setting into his hands.

At times like this, when I make myself, I can stand back and watch my mind sprinting toward disaster. *God, what a lot of separation anxiety I have*, that's what I see when I watch. *I should get over it.*

We're going to be having a lot of flooding, since a river runs under the house. Something else we didn't know. It's not that we have much of a basement to protect, but we do have the USS *Voyager* warp drive down there, blinking and humming – that million-dollar powerhouse of water filtration gear that's hitched to the plumbing underneath the house.

"You'd need to build an aquifer, I think," Charlie says.

An aquifer. I imagine it in silver, glass perhaps, reflecting a little light. Can you fill it with flowers?

There's a pause. "I think I really mean you need to build a dam."

Are you going to build a dam? my friend Jill writes from Vancouver. *I imagine you with wooden shoes on, and one of those triangular white caps, growing tulips. Aren't there lots of dykes around already?*

⌐

When the charms are burned, the sick usually change for the worse; so that often they utter terrible cries and roars. The sick utter the most mournful sighs without any manifest cause.
– Francesco-Maria Guazzo, *Signs of Maleficia* (1626)

She knows about Zelda. *I wish you well*, she says, but she's practical too. She knows that trappings can help, so she's given me her geraniums, the huge grandmotherly ones potted up in the house where they've held court in the best windows for years. I had a grandmotherly one myself that Zelda gave me, way back when, and it didn't survive the move from Vancouver. *Take these in remembrance of me, replacement of her*, Carol might have said.

She knows I'm going to be alone. But she's alone too, soon to be quite alone, and her own situation captivates her more. I can't expect her to spend her energy on me, and she doesn't. She expects me to take it on the chin, to hold the flame beneath my palm; she expects me to proceed as if I can make a difference, to count down from ten but not too far, to number how I am today. She expects me to be hardened off.

Don't cry, she said when she told me, that first time two months ago. *Don't you dare cry, don't you make me cry too.* Crying was all she wanted me to do, of course, and all she wanted to do herself, and we both knew it, but she's always been better at discipline than me. She's methodical. She's like a surgeon tying off bleeders. There'd been a brilliant sky god streaming through the clouds over Diamond way back in September when we arrived, after the gale and the day before we knew her awful news, and it had been on my mind to tell her when we next spoke. But then she called with her news, and I put it aside. There's not been another since, and I'm glad of it, since I couldn't tell her now either.

She has her own well-wishers. Everyone is a well-wisher when you're sick, sending cards and hope, but when you're dying the wishing changes shape, ominously. The smiles of the well-wishers are bright as ever; it's the wish that turns dark and oppressive. *Get in line*, it says. *Bear up. Deal with it.* Everyone from the doctors on down to her family and friends is possessed suddenly of the idea that she should *die well*, that she should die happy, that she should have a *good death*.

We never saw anyone so stuck in the grieving process, say the nurses on the palliative ward.

Euthanasia – from the Greek for *good death* – is what it takes to die well. Literally. We don't know our etymology any longer, Nick used to say, or we wouldn't say the stupid things we do. Nick has a classical education and loathes pop culture. She reviles inexactness or laziness or just plain mistakes in speech, and seems to have the *Oxford English Dictionary* inscribed on a flick file in her head. It irritates her to hear newscasters talk about countries decimated in wars when they mean devastated, laid waste. To decimate means to take out every tenth one, she'd point out. From the Latin *decem*, ten.

There's an art, apparently, to dying before your time, a political correctness to it. Nowhere in North America does it involve euthanasia, the true *good death*, except in the state of Oregon where there are still so many hoops for dying patients to jump through that most expire while they wait for clearance. Palliative care is founded on the politically correct, polite approach to death. No one should rage against the dying of the light any more. Instead, we should all step smartly through the five stages of Elisabeth Kübler-Ross's *On Death and Dying. Denial and Isolation. Anger. Bargaining. Depression. Acceptance. A-one and a-two and a . . .*

•

Hannah Gruen is the housekeeper. She's helped raise Nancy since Nancy's mother died when she was three. Hannah loves Nancy as a daughter, but is not quite up to Nancy's or her father's speed. She cooks good food and goes to church.

Palliative care was a surprise to me. I had thought it would be entirely different, a place of succour where, finally, we could be ourselves, agony and anguish and mortal warts and all. I'd assumed that here, at last, was a place for truth, a place where we could take the kitchen table apart, night after night; where we could disclose, say how it was without pretence or expectation.

Carol was in agony. Why could no one see that? Why wouldn't they?

Doctors are largely indifferent to palliative care. There's little scientific challenge to it after they get the mix of palliative drugs right, and death seems to thumb its nose at science and medicine anyway. Only the coroners are impresarios of death; poking through the dead, they can still bend their spoons, palm their aces, do their tricks. Carol sees one of the two oncologists that still practise in the province, but not until a full month after she's first admitted to hospital. They screen the cases referred to them and pick only a few, so most cancer patients never see one at all. Medical specialties are getting scarce here, only pairs of them remaining as if we're all packing for Noah's Ark. Only two ophthalmic surgeons have lasted and very few ophthalmologists, so she never gets to see someone about the changes to her vision her drugs have caused, as well as what's been caused by the cancer itself. There still seems to be a reasonable complement of psychiatrists, however – you can get to see one for an hour every three weeks – and she asks for one. But she never gets referred, and she never learns why.

The oncologist writes her out a drug regimen, furrows his brow a few times during their brief conversation, then hurries away. Has death bested him? Does he wish he could shove all its yapping in a drawer, as Mr. Drysdale does with the phone in *The Beverly Hillbillies* when his wife, Margaret, calls him at the bank?

Does death embarrass medicine, shame it? Is that why the hospital staff say all the right things but still seem a little distant, a little condescending? We get distant too, the rest of us, a bit stunned, a bit perplexed. Death makes fools of us all, makes us shake our heads in bewilderment when we realize it. It makes all our practice at affirmation and self-realization and eating right and sunscreening and anti-oxidizing and expressing our anger in positive ways – makes all our running after good health and long life look a little silly, or at best, a little short of the goal.

We get lost too. There's no one in the world who cries out more for help than the one who is dying, even the silent one who has built her will over a candle flame, *in me an invincible whatever*, and in a hospital there's not a place in the world where help's less possible. Often when I see her I feel I'm in a closet, and that I need to step out in order to draw near and help. If I can just make it out of the closet I'll find myself in a room where there are white blinds filtering strong sunlight, where there are folded white towels and bandages in rolls and vials of restoratives stacked on white shelves, and most of all a sink where we can scrub everything down and start over. But instead the room beyond the door is just another dark closet with four bare walls, no sink, and a door that leads back into this one.

When she's admitted for the last time, the palliative care nurse comes and sits by the corner of her bed, smooths her sheet, tries to take her hand. Carol pulls back. She doesn't know this woman from a hole in the ground. Why should they hold hands?

"Do you like a little something after dinner?" the nurse asks.

We stare at her.

"Wine? A liqueur? It makes some people feel a little better."

It's true. No one had noticed that she hasn't eaten for weeks, or realized that if she can't tolerate food she certainly can't tolerate drink. No one noticed, either, that she's cried and cried for drift drugs, for relief from her anguish, for anything that might make her feel a little better.

Carol has to find her own way, and no one likes it when she does. She's dying young. It's a senseless death. Someone has killed her by glancing away, by cramming his schedule, by washing his hands of her. In the time that's gone by since he overlooked her, he's forgotten her altogether. Her way of dying is an angry way, bitter and frustrated, overwhelmed by injustice, loss, and grief. How could anyone imagine it could be otherwise? But everyone does.

Some nights B collects me from the hospital and tries to take me away from it all. But at the Cineplex it's death all round as well.

Arnold Schwarzenegger's latest blow-'em up, *The End of Days*.
Gentle things like *Dogma*, about angels among us and a modern,
sweet God, Alanis Morissette doing a handstand in plaid boxers
and a Christian LaCroix bustier. Stephen King's *The Green Mile*,
about a pet mouse on death row. Do we so fear death that we have
to mount it huge, in 70mm colour and Dolby Sound, populate it
with cute mice, and screen it with popcorn? It's as if we take
revenge on others because our own time's cut short. It's as if in
blowing everyone up in tiny pieces, in every Hollywood way imag-
inable, we feel ourselves gel and grow more solid. *It's happening
to them up there on the screen, wow, is it ever happening to them.
It isn't happening to me.*

"He let me return it no problem," she'd told me in September.
"He said there, there. Dear, dear. No problem, no *problem*." She
was talking about the clerk in the shoe store where she returned
the shoulder bag she'd bought just before she found out. "I think,"
she'd concluded, "that everyone's just so damn glad it's not happening to them. They'd do anything for me, just to keep it away
from them. They'd do anything, period."

Over the phone, she'd even laughed a little at that. It all seems
such a long time ago now, that laugh. "This guy in particular, he
yelled at the other clerk to put the bag away in the back even before
I was out the door. She was a lot younger, maybe she was new, he
was completely mean to her. I think it was just to show that he
could, to test his strength, to show that he still had it."

Is it really a very long way back to the Coliseum? And yet when
we talk about death – we sensitive, educated ones, at least – we
talk about celebrating it. Which is it, fear or celebration?

Or is it just an awful, ancient sadness we can't shake?

Who can run the race with death? asked Dr. Johnson. Carol

seems to die both too fast and too slow. Too fast because she's young yet to be snatched away; too fast because she barely has time to take in the news before she's gone. Too slow because since she's had too little time, she'd have been better having no time at all. *Let me die in my sleep*, we all say. *Let me go fast*. "One should always have one's boots on, ready to leave," said Montaigne. "I want death to find me planting my cabbages, but caring little for it, and much more for my imperfect garden." Too slow because when there's no future there's no context any longer, no meaning in anything. There's nothing here for her now, and there hasn't been for nearly a hundred days.

When I count it up, it makes me stare. It has been a race, after all, and we've both lost.

•

I've been to see her. She's barely there. She's sick, she's sick, she's dying. I've stroked her face. Her skin is taking on a hue and mottling as the blood vessels break down. I'm emptied of my senses when I'm with her, my eyes are constantly wet and murky, but I see that. I've been watching for it.

A doctor has been cruel to her. They're trying to convince her to leave the hospital and go into a nursing home, to unhand the hospital's budget. *You could go on for two years like this*, the doctor has told her, exasperated. *Who knows?*

No. No. No, Carol whimpers. It's the last thing I ever hear her say.

You're dying now, Carol, I tell her, as if it's good news. But she won't listen to me. She's always listened to doctors, too much. *No. No. No.*

The highway under the car reels out beneath us like night ice off Greenland, into black waters we can't see.

We get home late. The moon is high and bright. It washes us, lights the snow with diamonds. I feel completely emptied, cleaned out as if I'd vomited and vomited but I'm stopping now. Perhaps it's the expectation of release, perhaps it's denial, who knows: suddenly I love it here, even for just a second. It's the first such second I've had.

It's beyond lovely. Stretches and stretches of white and silver and diamonds in the night.

[FIVE]

Soup

It was a bad time for her to die, in the grey days of winter. I walk the Diamond farmhouse, from room to room. Then the Diamond fields, meadow to meadow. It occurs to me the farm should be diamond-shaped, like a ballfield. Fleet of foot, I should progress from base to base to base. A little struggle, a little sweat, and finally I should hit the comforts of home. Instead, it's shapeless, an amorphous *via dolorosa* with borders that float. They swim away, demand more effort to walk on days when I'm tired. And that's almost every day.

There've been a hundred of these days altogether. A hundred days since she was diagnosed, and then she died.

As Dr. Johnson wrote to Mrs. Thrale back in the 1700s, grief is a species of idleness. Dr. Johnson was merciless, not much of a hand-holder. He's known for the kinds of barbs he wrote to Boswell: *Are you sick, or are you sullen?* Vowing no kinship to sickness, sullenness, grief nor idleness, for long days I don't know what to do with myself. I walk and walk. No one who walks like I do can be sick, or idle.

We've had a dusting of snow over the farm. Looking out the bedroom windows over the tops of Carol's hibiscus blooming on the sills, I note the hoarfrost on the old plank bridge over the stream, the frozen stream itself, the dusted shingles on both barns, the fencing to the fields beyond, where the deer venture out from the woods, and the way the frosted tree branches brush the window, framing it all. I note all this, think it extraordinarily beautiful, and think it possible the malaise of the last hundred days might one day lift.

⁕

It's early in the morning, but the hospital is awake. It's not slept any better than I have. I'm truly sleep-deprived now: in the last weeks, at her house and then when we return here, I'm often up all night. It makes me hungry. When her breakfast comes, I down the banana, toast, and tea while she sleeps. I don't like milk in my tea but I add it in now, I'm that hungry. She's still sleeping when lunch comes. I think I recognize the blob of white lumped onto the plate. It might be chicken.

Sawing it into bits, I think of Nick. I think of Nick a lot these days, her bon mots, her gaffes. She used to say the most outrageous, hurtful things, and sometimes the wisest things too. She used to call me Beauty. In my worst moments she'd stroke my head, call me Old Thing.

This is the kind of day she'd call me Old Thing.

What I'm thinking about now is food. Nick used to say that as women get toward the end of their lives, they should live together and eat out of the same pot.

She was reared on culture, civility, history. She used the finest of her china for breakfast, lunch, and supper whether she had guests or not, and she was always buying it too. Nick always used her best things. Even the kids got their juice in cut-glass tumblers. But she was a terrible cook, chopping last-minute hunks of raw onion into sauces where they should've stewed all day, making custard pies that never set, spooning it all out on her latest eight-place setting of Mikasa.

Nick's sister had trained as a concert soloist, and Nick knew the repertoire. She'd sing from *Dido and Aeneas* as you worked alongside her in her garden, helping her paint her study, making cranberry cakes with her at Christmas. God knows, someone had to help her get the Christmas cakes right.

> *When I am laid, am laid in earth*
> *May my wrongs create no trouble, no trouble*
> *In thy breast*
> *Remember me! Remember me.*
> *But ah! Forget my fate, forget my fate.*

"What do you mean, morbid?" Nick would say. "It's sublime."

I can imagine eating from Nick's pot at the end of our lives. She'd keep us entertained and outraged. She'd keep us in good dishes. She'd keep us thin.

We should be together at the end of our lives. Yes, we should. Our men will have left us alone, one way or another. We ought to be alone together. Picture a Cape Cod in white clapboard, a sturdy house with a garden rolling down to the sea from a broad veranda.

Picture a great many windows, and not many stairs. On the veranda in their rockers sit three or four old dolls, grey, desiccated,
arguing, laughing, picking at the stockings wrinkling on their
ankles, smoking, drinking, watching birds. But especially smoking
and drinking, all of us who'd given both up. It hardly matters now.

We'll have cats, even a dog if we want one. We'll carve huge
ghoulish pumpkins at Hallowe'en and label the goodies we give
out with our address: *The Dolls' House*. We'll be dotty, reeking,
tipsy. Everyone will love us. We'll make sure Nick doesn't make
the Hallowe'en treats.

Carol won't be there.

·⟶

In Vancouver, my friend Jill has a dinner party. Cream of potato,
leek and watercress soup; green salad with Roquefort dressing;
rabbit in Dijon sauce with roasted potatoes and carrots; a pie with
a blackberry coulis made from berries in her garden. It's the kind
of party she's renowned for, the kind I miss now. At Diamond, if
you don't make it, you don't eat. You can't just send out for Thai.

There are expanses of dirty dishes after Jill's party, and when
her guests spill onto the street at one in the morning, she follows
them. She wants to get some air before she starts cleaning up. She
stands for a minute, drinking in the air, enjoying the night. And
then she hears a bird sing. There are no nightingales on the west
coast, no nightbirds that she knows of, but there it is, a sweet song,
a bustle in her hedgerow. She can hear it clearly during the lulls in
the traffic. She follows the song to a tree down the block, but as
she approaches, it stops. Perhaps the bird has flown; perhaps it's
sitting very still, thinking *Danger*. But she can't see it, can't find it.

Has she made it stop? Had it been singing out of panic, in a sort of bird night madness that comes with finding yourself caught in the lights of the city when you should be in the dark of the woods? Can it have been an escapee, a tropical caged bird singing its last? She'll never know.

In medieval France, Mother Staunton of Wimbish was refused milk by Robert Cornell's wife,

> *whereupon she sat down upon her heels before the door and made a circle in the ground with a knife.*
>
> *After that, she digged it full of holes with the compass, in the sight of the said wife, her man and her maid, who, demanding why she did so, she made answer that she made a shitting house for herself after that sort, and so departed. The next day the wife coming out at the same door was taken sick, and began to swell from time to time as if she had been with child; by which swelling she came so great in body as she feared she should burst, and to this day is not restored to health.*

Jill has been sick again. She thinks it's something she ate. Maybe the chocolate cake. And just in case it was, she'll never eat chocolate cake again.

Really? Chocolate cake could kill me, I tell her, and I'd still eat it again.

Jill works as a food stylist on movie sets in Vancouver. She says hi to people like Sean Penn and Ben Affleck. She sees Jack Nicholson across a crowded room, and Sam Shepard too. She doesn't actually see Sam Shepard, the set's so stuffed with actors and famous people, but she knows he's there, he was on her list.

Jill can make watermelon peacocks and watermelon whales. It's easy, she assures me. Wasn't it Rodin who said that he let the people out of the stone? Jill lets the peacock out of the watermelon, it's apparently that simple. The watermelon becomes the body of the peacock, and the tail is long skewers of fruit stuck into the back. She makes fruit hedgehogs too, out of melons with skewers of fruit stuck into them all over. All the fruit's for two six-foot tables that will also be loaded up with drink fixings and flower arrangements. She does miniature Vietnamese spring rolls that are actually all wrapping with no filling, because it's a movie; chick peas on banana leaves; rice noodle salad; and green papaya with more fruit salad. For edible food for the extras, there's Japan rice crackers, fruit, and raw vegetables. She hopes the extras won't go through too much edible stuff. Extras should be experienced enough to look like they're guzzling drinks and gobbling food without actually doing it.

Jill knows exactly what to make a muffin out of when you want to blow it up. She can brown a turkey with a blowtorch. She has two fridges in her kitchen, and the tops of her kitchen cupboards hold stacks and stacks of large Rubbermaid storage boxes with lids. Jill goes through a lot of food, and she calculates quantities in ways that would surprise you. If a scene calls for two people eating dinner, each with a roll on a side plate, Jill will bring at least a couple dozen rolls to the set. It's for continuity, she explains. What if each actor takes a single bite out of his roll but the one scene in which they take that bite is shot six times, seventy-six times if you're working with Stanley Kubrick?

Jill banks a lot on food; she dreams about it. During the fruit shoot she dreams about mushrooms, lots of them growing by a path. She hopes to find chanterelles but doesn't. Every time she thinks it's chanterelles she's seeing, they turn out to be something else.

When I was four or five we lived for a while on Rectory Street in a small town in the Annapolis Valley called Bridgetown. There seemed to be no rectory on the street and certainly no church, but at the top of Rectory Street, on the corner where it intersected Main Street, stood a big turreted green house where the LeBruns lived. Though there must have been a bunch of them in a house that size, on a corner lot in a small spacious town, I have no recollection of any LeBruns other than Mrs. LeBrun. She was an invalid of some kind. My mother used to make an eggnog every morning and take it up to her in a tall crystal glass, on a crystal plate with a doily. My mother wrapped a linen napkin around the glass.

Jill's chocolate cake episode is only one in a series of stomach upsets. She's been sick for a while now, and she struggles to carve her whales and feather her peacocks and get to her shoots. From the east coast, I sit down and write her whenever I can, just for moral support. *Writing you mornings*, I tell her, *I feel like I'm bringing you your eggnog.*

There's something about food; women bring it. It's what they do. Watch for it in any movie or TV show where men are doing something important, and you'll see it's true – women are bringing men food.

My mother used to have a "how-to" book of cut-up animal birthday cakes for kids. You'd make a slab cake that, following the diagrams in the book, you'd carve to yield a trunk plus legs, a neck, a head, paws. You'd make seven-minute frosting, or boiled frosting as it can be called, and tint it with food colouring, then use a lot of toasted coconut – especially for the collar and cuffs of the lion cake. The lamb cake had white seven-minute frosting and a gumdrop eye, and was dotted with multicoloured Lifesavers. That one was splashy and loud, a Jean Paul Gaultier sort of cake for the Paris runways, or maybe even an Alexander McQueen. There was a yellow butterfly cake that had curled licorice strips for antennae. There were Mickey and Minnie Mouse faces too. You used chocolate wafers for their ears.

Women bring food for women too. My mother used to say that when I didn't eat she'd know I was at death's door.

There is hope, Anne Sexton wrote. *There is hope everywhere. Today God gives milk, and I have the pail.*

⁕

Nancy has a very beautiful home – a large brick house away from the street with a nice garden surround. On the first floor, there's a living room with wooden furniture, big chairs, a piano, and a large fireplace; a dining room; a library with bookcases, a large desk and a leather chair; and a kitchen. On the second floor are her father's bedroom, Nancy's own bedroom with TV and telephone, a bathroom with dressing table, Hannah Gruen's bedroom, Hannah's sewing room, and a guestroom.

Our last days together are terrible. Finding peace nowhere, looking for it everywhere, Carol shuffles between the hospital and home. Worse, she thinks leaving one place will swallow it up forever, like Brigadoon, so that she can't get back if she needs to. It's happened to her already. When they sent her home from the hospital the last time, they said not to worry, she could come back whenever she needed to. She needs to now, and she's having a hell of a time getting the okay.

I'll be her full-time caregiver while we wait, wherever we are, I tell her over the phone. I find out what she's still eating: nothing very much, maybe a little soup. "I'm putting the pot on as we speak," I tell her.

"Always throw a little barley in my soup," she reminds me. It's like her, the fibre and the instructions both.

I come to the city bearing two gallons of soup, one turkey vegetable, the other pea, spooned into a vast assembly of old vitamin and pill bottles. They were the tiniest containers I could find. I pack them like a little Lego high-rise into her deep-freeze. One of these, warmed in the microwave along with some milk, sits in front of her now in a dessert dish, untouched. She does sip at the milk, which I've frothed. We're at our wits' end: we don't know where to go any more. We enumerate the benefits of each place: hospital, home.

Hospital: they know how to care for you there, I say. I don't, that's for sure. I've been at this homecare thing for only a day so far, but already I'm exhausted.

No frothed milk there, she says.

When she'd gone to the hospital earlier, I'd packed her small milk mug, the size of a teacup in a child's tea set. When she saw it, she made me put it away in her bedside table lest it get broken. There's no pleasing her.

Now, the Economizer with the Groucho Marx eyebrows has finally sent her home to die. He packed off a set of instructions with her – that she should nest among the things she'd made a home of, the things she loved, the trimmings that had pleased her and protected her when she was well. She should enjoy the time she had left.

Who thinks this stuff up, anyway? A week, a day, an hour with Carol in her catastrophe dispels the romance we've built up lately around death. There's no nostalgia to her home any longer. She doesn't see the paintings and the plants, the bevelled oak doors and the antique brass pulls she chose for the kitchen cupboards in the new addition, the tweedy fleck in the carpet, the collection of cranberry Depression glass on a bookshelf.

She sees how many steps it will be to the bathroom, how hard it will be to turn in bed.

One of the terrible things about Carol's end is that there has been nothing at all uplifting about it – no Hallmark moments, no glimpsed wisdom, no galvanized courage. No family gathered, no soft lights, no whispered reconciliations, no unspoken understandings, no lace curtains lifting on the breeze at the window, no Tuesdays, no Morrie. She's dying a mistake, a victim of a bad joke – about a doctor, perhaps, who was at the bottom of his class in med school.

She's always had an unhappy life. This she carries to her death. She is anguished. Every moment is a moment of terror. She is dragged to the slaughter.

I check to see what of her home might still register on her, on Carol, the doyenne of gracious living, the brilliant cook, the master decorator, the cheerful scrubber, polisher, and vacuumer, the perfect hostess, the resourceful friend. I look round the breakfast room.

"What do you still care about? Anything? Yvonne's dishes?" Her friend, a production potter, had made her an eight-place setting of stoneware for Christmas years before. It's slate, sturdy, elegant. My turkey soup is congealing now in one of Yvonne's dessert dishes.

"Pffft."

I'm surprised she can still *pffft*, that she has strength enough left even for derision. "Why'd you ask for it for your soup, then?"

"Right size. Egg cup's better but it could tip." She cleans the frothed milk out of her cup with a fingertip. Every movement's so slow I'm nearly stopped too, feeling at odds with time, my thought and action out of sync as it is when I'm walking in cold so dire I can't speak without slurring, sounding drunk.

"Yvonne? Do you still care about her?"

"Love Yvonne. Always will, dead or alive. You too. Don't need to stick around for that. Either of you. Abstract." There's a long pause, one of those dark, black, wide-eyed, drug-induced stares. "You know?"

I think I know. I try again.

"You don't look at the blooms on the gardenia and think, *nice*?" In this I surely had a winner. We'd slaved over that damned gardenia, ferried it back and forth between the two of us several years ago to see who could get it going again. In the end, she had, and now it frothed its white blooms over her kitchen windowsill.

"I note them." Her voice, her face, is flat.

She had to starve it to get it going, fool it into thinking it would soon be gone and had better produce some bloom and seed for another generation before it went. The gardenia is perhaps the one thing in nature that does well when starved.

⁓

She insists I use one of their cars. There'll be prescriptions to pick up, errands to run. John gives me the metallic-blue Sprint, not the metallic-green Golf. When he shows me where things are on it he holds the key out of reach, as if I can't be trusted driving a Tonka truck through a sandbox.

"You're awfully hard on him," B says when I report in. "You'd worry about lending someone your car too."

But I'm hard on everybody. Nothing suits me, no one pleases. I'm angry with everyone – B himself, for instance, for calling too little while I'm staying with Carol, or for calling too much. And as irrational as it is, I'm angry with her too.

But if I'm angry, so is she. She rings the bell to summon me in the middle of the night. I fight my way up from the depths of sleep, reel down the stairs, alarmed. What can it be? She's lying there, picking at her bedspread. "Untidy, bedside tray," she says. "Straighten it? Can't lie here a minute more, looking. State it's in." She scowls, as if this is something I should've taken care of before lights out.

In the thin light of the lamp I look at all her prescription bottles in their cookie tin beside the bed, at the sedatives in particular. She takes so many that she needs an elephantine dose now to knock her out, and another shortly after to keep her there. Just now, at four in the morning, awakened and summoned to tidy a table, I want to pour them down her throat. I smile, though, reassure her. I straighten the damn table. We talk in whispers, as if there's still someone left to wake up. I work on the hem of one of her hooked rugs. I sit with her till she drifts, an hour, two. I'm a bad sleeper at the best of times, and these are not the best of times. Once I get back to bed, it's another hour before I fall asleep.

And then a knock at my door, polite. Another, persistent.

"Yes?" The clock reads 8:30 on the nose. I've been back to sleep a half an hour. I could burst into tears.

John pushes open the door, Jeeves-like, stands there with a tray. "I've got you a cup of tea here, and one of those lemon cookies you like so much. No hurry, though. No hurry at all to get up. Carol told me you were up in the night."

I can't decide whether he's a troll under a bridge, or simply an Englishman with impeccable manners who's under a great deal of stress. Whichever it is, sharing living quarters with him is not working out. We've begun fighting over how he will care for her; soon, he cares for me too, and I don't like it any better.

"Please, *please* don't feel you have to feed me," I'd implored him when I first arrived. "The idea isn't that you should have to look after me on top of looking after Carol. The idea is we'll both look after Carol, me in the day while you're at work, and both of us at night, and I'll look after myself."

"But it's not often we have *guests*," he said. He smiled his smile.

I get Carol her meals, her quarter pieces of toast and her thimbles of milk. But before I'm back up the stairs to the kitchen he's bringing me mine, and toast and tea between them, everything on a tray with a proper linen napkin. I'm well-fed; I'm exasperated. When I try to jump the gun on him by starting dinner myself, he seizes the broom and sweeps the kitchen floor furiously around my feet. He looks at the fish I've got started in the pan, then at the carrots going into the steamer.

He's dismayed. "That only takes a few seconds," he says of the fish. His tone's not nice.

"And so do the carrots." I bite my lip, but not enough. "I've done this before once or twice, you know, John," I say. I dig down hard at the frying pan bottom with a fork. It'll be the second Mrs. Wilcox's frying pan soon enough: who cares if I gouge it?

He tells me to watch out for the shower in the upstairs bathroom; the hot water's really hot. "I so seldom have to remember it any more," he says. "It's so seldom we have *guests*."

"Why don't you turn it down?"

"Turn it down? We don't want to turn it down. We like our hot water hot." He smiles his smile. "Why? How do you like yours?"

Cold, I want to say. *I like my hot water cold*. Whatever will placate him, make him feel he's won, that there's never been a game, that I'm not here and never have been and never will be again. These few homecare days I spend with Carol feel like I've been injected onto the set of *Long Day's Journey Into Night*. She's irritable to me and unkind to John. I see it, he sees I see it, and it seals my fate. He's an Englishman, after all, as is God, and his pride's been damaged. My being there at all has done that already, quite without Carol having at him every minute. I've invaded his territory, taken away his prerogative, perhaps even shown him up as an imperfect caregiver. He wants me out of there, and he works toward the purpose.

"You'd think," says B on the other end of the phone I've pulled away to a private corner to cry into, "that people would be especially nice to one another when one of them's dying. You'd think they'd be on their best behaviour."

But I think people act worse under stress, not better.

Her time at home revolves around dread of her bladder. Cancer brings on a particular complication called cachexia. From the Greek for *bad condition*, it's the wasting of famine, along with crippling weakness, metabolic disturbances, and ongoing loss of appetite. Once it was thought that a tumour stole nutrients from its host parasitically, but now it's known that certain cancers and even the patient's own white blood cells can produce cachectin, a hormone that depresses appetite centres in the brain. Perhaps Carol's own defences are backfiring in a vain attempt to starve her tumour by shutting down her appetite. Whatever its mechanisms, cachexia has by now so weakened her that she can't walk or even stand on her own. Getting to the bathroom is exhausting. Thinking about it is worse, for both of us.

Maybe it's time to go back to the hospital, I say. But she doesn't know, she can't decide, and the days are an endless round of calls to the nurses who befriended her during her earlier stays and to the doctors who didn't, a parade of opinions as to the location of some fictional place where everything will be all right. *The heart of Diamond, the heart of Diamond* – in the rocker by the head of her bed I find myself moving to the pulse of it. It's a way of not hearing her conversations. It's not that I don't want to hear her – it's the silence or the dodging or the irritation or the downright disdain on the other end that I can't bear. When she sleeps between phone calls, I turn the pages of a TV *Guide* from three months before. It's dated early September and laid down beside my chair, next to the TV, still open to Sunday's listings. It's as if time stopped for Carol and John that Sunday. She began her tests on the Monday. I lay it down, cast an eye over the colours of this renovated basement room, the fading folds of the cropped drapes at the basement windows. It's dim, panelled, hung with her rugs and fabric panels. But it's cozy, and visiting doctors and the VON have not known that to Carol, cozy is now more important than bright.

"Get her out of there and upstairs," they've said to me as if she should have no say in the matter, as if I could lift her in one hand

and the hospital bed in the other, as if a change of scene would make any difference.

"I'm talking about dying," she's said to them. "You're talking about making things pretty."

She wakes and makes more calls. Again, I carry her to the bathroom and back. I really think you should go back to the hospital, I say, panting. But John disagrees. He doesn't realize it's not dials and vials and gadgets she wants, not techniques and tricks and strategies, but comfort and care. She wants to be understood, validated. In her last days now, she wants to be heard, she *wants* to be carried. She wants John to damn the doctors with her, beginning with the one who has so blithely killed her. But John is fixed on civility and solutions. He brings home a plastic bed sheet, the kind that makes you sweat, an econo-pak of a hundred "in-out" catheters, and a "female urinal." This is a large, squat plastic bottle with a long pinched neck that opens out to a sort of funnel. It looks like something you'd use in pickling, or to water your plants.

The sight of it is enough to drive anyone into hospital, and I pack her up to go back.

⌣

The cook's secret to soups and sauces: sauté the base vegetables first. Celery, carrots, onions, for example. Cook them gently on medium-low heat until they start to brown. This step can take at least thirty minutes. The slower the better! Then add liquid – wine, stock, or water – just a bit (maybe a quarter-cup), and scrape up the golden bits. Let this reduce, wait for it to start to brown again, and repeat as many times as you have the patience. The greater your patience, the deeper the layer of flavour you'll bring to your cooking. One caution: don't sauté and simmer garlic – it goes bitter. But peppers, shallots, tomatoes, leeks – all these work well. Most everything works well. You can make a delectable soup with two onions and all the faded vegetables at the bottom of the fridge.

We have Carol's squash soup for lunch. It's the only way B will eat squash, despite what I say about fibre and flavonoids. I peel, seed, and cube a large butternut squash, dice up two onions, a carrot, and a couple celery stalks, then smash as many garlic cloves as I can find under the blade of a knife. I'm out of patience today: no sautéeing. This all gets boiled up in chicken stock till it's mushy.

I've never used Oxo for this, Carol said. I'd wanted something special for the holidays, and she'd brought over a trial batch and the recipe. It had been snowing. As she came in the door, her pot lodged between two red-checkered oven mitts, a few downy flakes hung for a moment in her hair, making it blacker than ever. Her cheeks bloomed in the cold. It would've been the fifth last Christmas we shared, perhaps less: perhaps the fourth. So many things then we didn't know. It all seems so many years ago. She'll never know now, and I add a couple Oxo envelopes to the end of stock I've taken from the freezer. I purée it all in three blender loads, then stir in the cumin, curry, ginger, and cream.

B licks his spoon. "This is squash?"

⁓

She asks me what I think happens when we die. "What do the Buddhists think?"

Someone's given her a bracelet of Buddhist prayer beads, and I'd asked a Buddhist friend of mine to tell me about them. I take a stab at explaining the theory of non-attachment, sitting practice,

breathing, change and not-change, reincarnation, karma, dharma.
I pass on what a Rinpoche, a Buddhist teacher, is supposed to have
said about death: "You're here, then you're not. A cosmic joke of
the universe." They're laid-back, those guys.

It's safe to tell Carol a thing like that. She's never been sentimental. She's always wanted to know. *When you have information*, she used to say, *then you have something*.

For a long time she says nothing. Then, "And Christianity?
What do the Christians think?"

I reduce Christianity to a minute steak. Heaven, good works
versus faith, life as a dismal dress rehearsal for eternity at the right
hand of God.

And now, in the silence that follows, it's my turn. "What do you
think happens?" I ask her.

She's slower than usual to speak. "I think you live on," she says,
"in the people whose lives you've touched."

"That must be very comforting. You've touched a lot of lives."

"But?"

"But it's not really a way for *you* to go on. Me, I'm not evolved
enough to be satisfied with that. I'm too selfish. I want to last.
Literally. I want my legs and feet to be intact, even. I can't break
my attachment to anything – not the vase that gets smashed, not
the pet that dies, not my Carol, especially not my own life."

"That's nuts," she says. "You can't last."

"Maybe not. But I'm not the only one who wants it that way.
The whole of Christianity wants it that way too. And so they say
you rise up in heaven or after Armageddon or wherever. All that
sound of the last trump stuff. They're talking resurrection of the
body, you know, not some airy-fairy thing like consciousness rising
up, the soul floating away. That's your *bum* you're meant to be

sitting on at the right hand of God. The trumpet sounds and somehow you pull your arms back on and step back into your feet,
though these are shinier now and pinker than before, and will last
you a lifetime. No, an eternity. And then you meet up with everyone who's gone before, right down to Spot the family dog."

"So that's what you think you'll get."

"I should be so lucky. No. What is it that Noel Coward has
Amanda say in *Private Lives* – that dying's probably some dreadful merging with things? I imagine she's right." *Listen, Carol,* I
want to say. What is it she wants to hear? What do I want to
believe? *Listen. It's like you'll be on an airborne merry-go-round
with the plushest white horses in the world, you'll sink down into
the back of your horse and wonder how you ever left, the clouds
whirling by will just brush your cheeks, you'll go up and down in
time to the music and feel so blissy and be so blessed, you can eat
straight out of the fridge and watch cable TV. If the damn phone
rings in the middle of something, you don't even have to pick it
up. And whenever you want to you can look down and see the kids
and John. You can see what they're doing and whenever they need
help, or just an arm round the shoulder, you can reach down to
them – to all of us – and just touch our shoulders with your little
finger. WiwaR to WoduridaR. We'll know you're there, and soon
enough, anyway, we'll come up and ride the horses with you.* "A
dreadful merging with things," I say. "She's probably right."

When B picks me up I ask him what he thinks happens when
we die.

Unlike Carol, he's quick to answer. B never has to think about
these things. "It all goes really dark," he says, "and that's it."

"Really." I fasten my seatbelt. "And that's okay with you?"

"It's like I've got a say?"

"Wouldn't you like to see me again?"

"Well, I'd love to. But I think the prospects are slim."

"So you don't believe in life after death?"

"That's Sunday school stuff," he says. He starts the car. "You go to Sunday school, and then you go to Engineering school, and the Sunday school stuff all goes away."

·⸜

My mother believes in ghosts. She thinks that the spirit survives, or some energy – whatever you call it. She lost her parents long ago, and more recently one of her brothers. Jack, the youngest, was always downtrodden in her eyes, and she mourns him as deeply as her mother. She was very close to her mother, whom she lost young and needlessly. My grandmother had a heart attack in the small Newfoundland outport where the family lived, and died waiting for a seaplane to take her to hospital in St. John's. My grandmother was sixty-five; my mother was in her twenties and well into a bad marriage by then. Her mother seemed an essential in her life, the cornerstone – the only person on earth, if not exactly the last.

My mother prays to her mother and Jack now, if you can call it that. Really, it's more that what mattered in her life before still matters now: it has a presence. It would not stop having a presence if she wanted it to: for none of us will it leave. My mother thinks of her mother when the phone rings. Who knows what's on the other end of the line? Her mother, Jack too, can keep her from harm, or at least share in it. *Don't let that be a problem on the other end of the line. Oh dear God, what's this in the mail? Mom. Jack.* It's not a lot different than the way I call her myself, for sympathy at the end of a bad day.

As far as I can tell, my mother has acquired her belief in floating, incorporeal, but coherent swaths of energy – if she drew them I imagine they'd look like gauzy clouds, or gusts of white wind – because of an illness she had when she was first married. My father and my mother were living in a tiny one-bedroom apartment over an appliance repair store when my father's mother made her inaugural visit to the newlyweds. Nanny was given the bedroom for the duration of her visit, while my parents slept on a pullout in the living room. My mother was constantly tired, working a three-to-eleven shift at the hospital seven days a week to put my father through dental school. She was hardly less tired for Nanny's visit. It was tough homemaking in the flat, just for the two of them, and working all day too. And now Nanny. My mother cooked on a hotplate for two, now three. There was a tin oven that fit over top of the hotplate, and daily she struggled with that. Nanny wanted to go shopping everyday before my mother's shift. The two of them went out each morning, on the bus, and then my mother dropped Nanny back home and walked to work.

To save the bus fare, my mother walked everywhere. She was always tired. One night, she came home from her shift with vertigo and nausea. She took a dishpan to the pullout and vomited into it over and over again, while my father complained about the noise. Sick as she was, for once my mother didn't care about him. He was neither here nor there. But neither was she – suddenly she was floating just beneath the living-room ceiling while she watched herself below, curled around the dishpan and vomiting.

When she finally fell asleep that night, that wasn't the end of it. Every night for five nights afterward, she'd get into bed on the pullout and promptly drift up to the ceiling. There she'd be, day after day, at Simpson Sears with Nanny every morning poking through the packaged linens, and floating under the ceiling every night. Finally, she told herself no. She refused to stay on the ceiling, even for a moment, and it stopped.

It enlightens me, this story, to my mother's separateness from me. I haven't been a child for more than thirty years, and yet I continue to think of her largely in the context of me. But this event had nothing to do with me. She was her own person drifting there along the wallpaper, doing her loop-the-loops. She could have been a circus performer, an acrobat in tights and a pink tutu. She was her own person, making her own decisions about whether she'd stay, or whether she'd go.

It's an intimate moment, and so I tell her then about what I want when I die, about how I want to step back into my feet and legs.

"Oh, trade them for someone else's, surely," she says. "You've got my rotten legs, after all. I'd trade mine for Betty Grable's, so should you. Here's your chance."

·–

"Let's go to Zellers and set off the security alarms at the doors," I say to B. John and I have had our moment behind the scenes, finally, and he has prevailed. He's declared my job at Carol's side redundant and sent me packing. I'm dismissed; I'm home, dazed and free, and I feel like doing something rash. I have a wristwatch with a bracelet band that's apparently the same wavelength as the one recognized by the shoplifting surveillance systems of some major department stores, those sensors on either side of the doors that go off if you carry out a piece of merchandise that hasn't been neutralized by a cashier. I have to unhook my watch bracelet when

I shop in town at Zellers if I want to avoid everyone stopping and staring, but today I won't.

It's a long way to go to the mall, though, and B eyes me strangely, so I settle for getting my hair cut in the village instead. It feels just as rash, and just as liberating. That's the thing about being a woman – you can use your hair for therapy. *Very blonde*, I tell Fern. *White. Think Madonna.*

In the chair across the tiled salon floor, Louelle is gelling the head of the Joico salesman. It's Louelle, not Louella: I know, because I've asked. The Joico salesman is named Rick, as they usually are, and he looks the way they usually look as well – squat, a bit thick, in pleated chinos and loafers all of twenty-four and about five-foot-eight. With a different haircut, he'd be on the edge of nerdy, and probably was in high school before he got this job and felt he'd won himself a piece of the future. Louelle makes sure he's got the right haircut now, with bleached bangs and a bit of a stand-up, scattered crown that looks like Smike's after I've scratched his ears and rubbed his head from back to front. Louelle has doe eyes and blonde ringlets that make her look like a toddler's doll. She sucks in her cheeks in concentration as she works over him.

Rick is complaining to the other girls that Louelle's cut his hair with ridges. Laughter tinkles round the room, over the piles of magazines, down the sink drains. I wonder if these guys get their cuts and their bit of attention from the salon girls for free. I wonder if it's Louelle he sees when he goes home to his wife. I wonder if it's still the future that looks back at him in the mirror.

At the chair next to Fern's, Belle is sharing the secret of superior dressing with the entire salon, at volume. It's her husband's recipe, and the secret is to grate in some commercial hamburger buns since

they're a little sweet. Belle's husband could eat his homemade dressing morning, noon, and night, just spooned out from a pan in the
fridge and fried in a little Blue Bonnet. It has to be Blue Bonnet,
though. Not Imperial, that's not the same, not Parkay, and certainly
not Becel or Fleischman's. He'd do real butter now, if he could,
that's best of all. But he's trying to *watch out*. You know.

Is he the size of a small barn, then? asks the woman in Belle's
chair. Belle is herself the size of a small barn and is pouring out of
her stretch pants under her smock, which pulls and puckers under
her chunky arms and has seams straining everywhere. But her
husband, she says, is skinny like Don Knotts, and sings like him too.

No one says anything to that. No one is sure how Don Knotts
sings.

Belle leaves her client for a minute to come over and towel and
comb me, because Fern has been called to the phone. Fern is still
on the phone when Belle comes over a second time and sprays my
head and combs me again. I've dried out waiting for Fern and I
dread that Belle might take me over and finish the job. Her own
hair is coloured a shade of burgundy you'd use to bind books, and
coats her head like a bouffant helmet.

Fern is on the phone because half the village is calling to check
on her and to see how her husband is. Jimmy was taken ill after a
party the weekend before. They had only eight tickets between
them, Fern's explained to me, and it takes me a while to realize
she's talking about drink tickets and saying he hadn't drunk much,
that wasn't the explanation. He awoke the next day feeling sick,
with his arm and side in pain. Now he's in ICU under cardiac obser-
vation, where he can't smoke and the nursing staff is trying to limit
his Pepsi intake. Jimmy's internist is named Dr. Saviour, and I

wouldn't have believed it had I not known dentists in Halifax called Dr. Precious and Dr. Lovely.

Fern's days at the salon are long with this going on, but she's visited Jimmy every night since he's been in, driving the extra miles in the wrong direction from home, smuggling him in his Pepsi, staring at the tubes and cables knitting up his body in the bed. Tonight, she says, she's not going in.

Must be hard, I say, knowing Timmy's waiting for you at home, the dishes, Timmy's homework, the clothes for next morning –

Nope, she says, I just can't go.

At suppertime, I tell B about Fern's husband and Belle's. We're making Thai chicken curry with sweet peppers.

"I wonder if anyone's ever made curried turkey dressing," he says.

·⸜

The good ship *Hope* landed on the Pictou coast by Diamond in 1751, three or four years before the *Hector* brought its more substantial cargo of dour, downtrodden Scots who are usually remembered as the original settlers. The *Hope* discharged only six adults, twenty children, and three black servants, legal slaves, then sailed on and never looked back. It returned to England for another load, which this time it delivered to its usual port of call in Boston.

The little band's first winter in Nova Scotia was a tough one. The distinction between master and servant paled soon enough. They had scarce food, clothing, and shelter, and hardly made it through. In the worst of it, they travelled inland by foot the forty miles to the settlement of Truro, the children too, and hired themselves out as farmhands and labourers for a few days or

weeks on end. They were paid in potatoes and other staples occasionally, but mostly potatoes. These they dragged back to Pictou
on sleds, the lucky ones who had sleds, and those who did not
simply dragged their sacks behind them in the snow. There were
no roads then, no trails, just the tracks their potato bags made in
the snow.

Nadine McNamara is a self-styled psychic who lives down the
Diamond Road a ways from us. Two and a half centuries following the *Hope*'s departure from our shores, Nadine gets her fifteen
minutes of fame by predicting that volcanos will erupt in the
Atlantic and in the Bermuda Triangle, giving rise to a tumultuous
collision of Atlantic tsunamis. Things won't be helped, she says,
by the simultaneous ascension of the lost continent of Atlantis
from the depths of the ocean.

This was all to have happened two years ago on Saturday,
August fifteenth, and for the week leading up to it Nadine
somehow gets enough notice in the press that she's a national story.
Diamond alone will escape ruination, she says.

"Why, because it's slightly elevated?" I've been poring over B's
topographical maps.

"Nah, because she lives here," says Charlie.

While the national media more or less forgets about Nadine,
even on the fifteenth, locally the day comes and goes with much
fanfare. The weather is gorgeous. People mill about wearing the *I
Survived the Tidal Wave* T-shirts they've had printed up.

Our Hope is gone, the Scots might have said. *I Survived the First
Winter Anyway. I Survived the Tidal Wave. I Can Do It Again. I
Can Take Anything You Can Give.*

I see her the day before she dies. She lies on her side, a position she'd avoided for months to protect her swollen liver, and gurgles through her congested throat. Perhaps her new handlers at the nursing home don't know how to place her; perhaps they don't care. She's certainly past telling them. Her skin is tight across her face as if a hand has seized the back of her head and gathered up any give in the scalp, binding it, twisting it, not letting go. Her eyes bulge. Her lips are split and chapped. Now and then bubbles form on them, and are gone.

I sit for a time near the head of the bed, resting my chin on the side rail, holding her feverish hand in mine. Her hands and feet aren't gaunt like the rest of her, but swollen, as if she'd walked a long way and dragged herself the rest. I talk to her, I think.

"Can you feel your hand in mine?"

The barest squeeze, imperceptible. I might be imagining it.

"Okay, then, don't let go. Wherever you go, keep me with you."

I hang my head on the bed rail a long time. It's cold at first, but then it warms and I can no longer feel it, just something stiff against my temple, inchoate. The room around us seems to hang in space. She's been breathing this air for days now, and I suck it down into my lungs, send it out, suck it in. We used to share so many things. I loose her hand, rise eventually, walk to the door, step through it, swing it shut. It seems to me the door has closed on something monumental, something that would have spurted up and glowed if I'd looked round, something that might have vented a deep draft and pulled me back.

Her son's been sitting outside the door while I'm inside. He's got two coffees in Styrofoam cups, and there's a pile of creamers and sugar packets on his lap. "I didn't know what you wanted in yours," he says.

"Anything. Nothing." I hadn't wanted a coffee at all. It goes down black and thin and hot, twists my stomach when it hits.

Steven's pulling paper out of his pants pocket. It's an Excel chart of her drugs. He pushes it on me. "I did it on the computer," he's saying. For weeks I've had her drug regimen stamped on my mind, so that the barest glance at his page shows me a few stray decimal points in the dosages, a few misspellings. Like my B, like his father, John, Steven is an engineer. He takes comfort in *method* and *system*. It will be important to him that Carol's list of balms and poisons is finally in order, no longer scrawled in women's hand-writing, first his mother's and then my own. It will be important to him that he's taken the time to type it out, as if with typing will come understanding and, finally, peace.

But I want to have it less than the coffee. A lot less. "It's typed," I say stupidly. "Good." I hand it back to him.

He's due back at work soon, and he's got a flight out tomorrow. "I'll go with that," he says, "unless –" *Unless she dies in the night.*

I touch his shoulder. I leave as I began, without asking him how he is. Each time I've phoned the house over the last three months, I've started the conversation with his father by asking him how he is. "Fine," John would say brightly, invariably. "And you?"

I can't bear it any more. Chip off the old British block, what would Steven say today? "I'm a one. No, not even a point one." That's what I think he should say. What if he just shrugged and said, "Well, you know, about a five"?

In the common room, a nurse appears out of nowhere and accosts me with a long, unsolicited account of why they've stopped suctioning Carol's trachea. She sits across from me in denim over-alls, a large pack of Export 'A's glimpsing out of the bib pocket each time she leans toward me to make a point, or to demonstrate on her own trachea, or mine: "Here, here. Here's the point she'll gag on the tube. We don't want that."

My mind is back in the room. It'd been a week since I've seen her, and till then it had been a process of dead reckoning to know where we were, and how much longer we'd be there. She left us a little more each day; this we knew by plotting on from the last fix, as a ship would, on the basis of its course and speed. In the week I've stayed away, it's clear she's fairly flown through her dangerous waters. Had I not known her room number, I could have pushed open every door and never recognized her.

The nursing home John put her in seems full of old and not-so-old women tied down in wheelchairs. As I sit in the common room, one comes up and wheels herself right into my legs, bumper cars.

"Untie me," she says, looking up at me conspiratorially. "Help me get away."

"I can't," I say, looking down at my hands. It seems to be all I've been saying for months.

⁓

We stop at my mother's on the way home, taking the Christmas turkey frame with us for soup. It's been a tradition in my family for years – my mother cooks the turkey for Christmas Day; my sister gets the leftovers for casserole or quiche; and I get the frame for soup. Time was, my sister would distribute her casseroles back to us, and I'd pass out jars of soup. But now we live too far apart to feed each other, to eat out of the same pot.

We come back by way of the highway. It seems shorter for once, safer, after all the freezing rain. On the way, we pass an Irving station. A sign by the pumps says

HAPPY NEW YEAR

BAKED BEAN

"Who knows?" I say, to no one in particular. When we get back it's nearly midnight, and the farmhouse is an icebox. B starts a fire in the woodstove. Before I take off my parka, I put the frame of the bird into the soup pot, fill the pot with water from the Green Hill spring, and set it over a flame on the stove. I chop up an onion, then another. The pot boils and I turn it down. I stand there, over the bones of that year, well into the night.

•ᴗ

It's the day after she died. "After all this," I say to B at lunch, "what do you think it's all about, anyway?" We're having the soup from the all-nighter turkey frame. He's having it, at least. I'm stirring mine round and round in the bowl.

"What, life?" he says, looking queasy. He hates having to talk about such things; he's an engineer. But to humour me, he gives it a shot. "It's about finding a good woman and a great bowl of soup."

I've been looking a long, long time. I don't think I've found anything wiser or truer yet, or could put it any better.

•ᴗ

She asked me to write her obituary when the time came, so I send B over to her house to get her portfolio from John. I want to get all the dates right, the places, the titles of her awards, scholarships, accomplishments. I don't want a hair out of place. She never did in life; in death too, I'll try to protect her.

She'd told John she wanted me to do this job, but he says he doesn't remember, and is clearly not pleased that I do. It's a strange thing, the silent rancour that has sprung up between the two of us. Perhaps I simply got the brunt of all the anger they felt for one another.

At the top of her portfolio is a newspaper photograph above an announcement that she's been appointed to the job where I met her. There she is, ten years ago, looking up at me and smiling, in that same white lace collar she wore the day we unearthed one another. Her smile is dazzling. Her hair is so dark, her eyes too, and they sparkle. There's a tilt to her head. There's calm and polish. I stare at the picture a long time. It shocks me, at first, because I've forgotten what she looked like well.

I draft the obituary for John and wait to see what gets published. He's improved it some, adding a couple personal touches, but one thing he's added I can't abide. She died *peacefully*, he's written. He's injected a *peacefully* into my *she died January 2*.

Don't! I scream, to whoever can hear. I hold the newspaper high over my head and shake it so hard that the cats spring from the chairs where they've been sleeping and dart from the room.

B comes running. "Don't what? What the hell?"

"Don't tell lies about me when I can't rebut them. Don't tell lies about me just because you wish they were true. Don't you *ever* say I died *peacefully*. Say I died *miserably*, say I died *sullenly*, say I died laughing, say I died spitting in the face of God. Full of pain. Full of venom. Full of dinner, *full of shit!*, whatever." I'm screaming now, I'm shrill. "Full of *practice*, I'm getting so used to this, it's getting to be like taking a number at the post office and waiting for your turn to come up, or someone else's close to you. Full of rage. Yeah, that's it." I collapse into an armchair, wipe my mouth. "Say I died *full of rage*."

There'd been nothing peaceful about her death. Would she have wanted him to lie like this? Would she have wanted me to return the keys to the fortress to him, so that no one but me would ever know she hadn't died well?

Did he ever understand it, her illness, and her life or death either? *I'm tired of explaining things yet one more time* – she used to say that about him a lot, long before she got ill. She might have been talking about a trip they couldn't agree on taking, a call from her father, that stranger who'd become *Eileen and Bill*. The weight of the vacuum cleaner, perhaps, or the groceries in their bags and how she could use some help. Can it be that he thought her last few silent hours reflected a serenity she chose? Could he have mistaken her paralysis for calm, not understood that her breathing finally eased simply because her lungs couldn't work, her chest muscles couldn't move? You sink in secretions you can't cough out. Did he think she was smiling at him, not drowning?

. ᴗ

Carol's ring comes to me. I turn it over in my hand. *Now that you're gone, all that's left is a band of gold. All that's left of the dream I hold is a band of gold.* It's set all the way around with tiny diamonds. They represent steadfast love, always have. *And the memory of what love could be if you were still here with me.* Diamond is the ultimate gemstone, with a few weaknesses but many strengths. We all know it's the hardest thing. But it's four times as hard as the next hardest thing – corundum, the mineral that makes sapphire and ruby. How many of us know that, the nuances of hard?

I can't bury it now if I wanted to. The ground's frozen, and the brook by the house hasn't run in weeks. B's stopped stamping it open for the ducks, who sit in their barn like slug-a-beds talking amongst themselves, counting the dark days of winter. Perhaps they're telling Old Duck stories of the coming of the Dark Winter Duck, the invasion of the Ice Spirits and the flight of the Waters, and the eventual victory of the Sun Duck, who drives Winter Duck and his Ice Spirits from the land.

Our hope is gone, they might say, *but we survived the first winter anyway. In us, an invincible summer.* Spring will come. I'll decide what to do with the ring then.

It snows heavily over the farm for several days. The fields are too deep to walk. To waylay cabin fever and keep the driveway open, we get in the car and coast up and down between the house and the road, back and forth, back and forth. When the plough finally arrives to clear the Diamond Road, we drive up and down that too, just for the outing. The driving's better on the road in deep winter than in summer, because the potholes and the ruts are all filled with snow.

On the second day of the storm, I get up early to make soup, something light this time. We've been carrying too much weight all fall. Sweet potato and ginger: that's what I decide. It's one more way to hide another vegetable B thinks he doesn't like. *This is sweet potato?* he'll say, licking his spoon.

Yams, ginger root, stock, coconut milk, lime juice, almonds, coriander. Barley; Carol's barley. Should I throw in a little barley, for bulk? Once it's all assembled, I get it started on the stove and wander around the house. If I put on the stereo or even the pink Radio Shack transistor, I'll wake B, tuned as he is to airwaves of any kind. I fill the grinder with coffee beans and take it into the bathroom to run it, closing the door. Still nothing from upstairs.

I've been quiet enough, but the aroma of soup and coffee will wake him soon.

I hear a car, unusual enough for our little rickety unsigned stretch of the Diamond Road at any time of day, but unheard of this early, out of the question in this weather. I take the coffee grinder to the window. Beyond it there's nothing but snow, falling steadily on the fields, the barns, the driveway. But I hear the car still, and craning my neck I just see it then, far off in the distance, roaring backwards down the driveway straight and unerring as a bullet. It's taken a wrong turn in the storm, I'd say, and when it reaches the road it backs out and swings around. It's sparing no time; the pitch of the engine is high. I crane some more. It's a metal-lic-green Golf.

Behind me, the soup boils over on the stove. I run to turn it down, then run back to the window. Nothing. No sound, no Golf. No tire tracks at all in the falling snow. Three deer, Everett sur-vivors, have their heads down in the east meadow, worrying the grass through the snow.

The aroma of sweet potato and ginger soup fills the house.

·

On the last day of the storm the light falls in the late afternoon; the sky is dulled pewter. Something moves, near the barn. Anything stirring in the persistent white is conspicuous, and already I've sighted two tiny brown mice running for cover from the storm. That's led to a heated argument between us about whether or not B can put traps in the barn and in the greenhouse.

The weather's made me cranky. "Can't we just let something live for a change?" I yell at him, throwing my book on the floor.

Now, the dark smudge flitting alongside the barn materializes into a bird – not the brash, glamorous blue jays so profuse around the farm whatever the season, but a single nondescript sparrow. It sits for a long minute on a fence post, bobbling its head. Then it's gone, launched toward the west, and something turns in my throat as it goes. *What is the sound of one bird leaving?* I'll never see it again. Framed briefly in the cold, dank dusk, that small murky bird seems to me the bitterest sight in the world.

And yet I can imagine some country, far to the west and far beyond the sunset, farther than anyone could walk or sail or fly, a country whose bounds will recede in direct proportion to any approach. But one where a bird can enter, and Carol can enter, and everything we've lost. It's green there, and warm, the sun streams in. It's a place where they can go forever, and wait, and see who else turns up.

C